A CREATIVE APPROACH TO THE CLASSICAL PROGYMNASMATA

Writing & Rhetoric

BOOK 4: CHREIA & PROVERB

PAUL KORTEPETER

Writing & Rhetoric Book 4: Chreia & Proverb
© Classical Academic Press®, 2014
Version 1.2

ISBN: 978-1-60051-242-1

Classical Academic Press
515 S. 32nd Street
Camp Hill, PA 17011

www.ClassicalAcademicPress.com

Series content editor: Christine Perrin
Series editor: Gretchen Nesbit
Illustrations: Jason Rayner
Book design: Lenora Riley
Speech bubble icon courtesy of frankdesign/Vecteezy.com.
p. 78: Photograph of statue of King Alfred in Wantage Market Square courtesy of Steve Daniels via wikipedia.org.

Chreia & Proverb

TABLE OF CONTENTS

A Typical Teaching Week

Veteran teachers know that rarely is there anything typical about a teaching week. These guidelines are intended to help bring some predictability to lesson planning. Although the parts of speech and other elements of grammar are important aspects of this course, its primary focus is writing and rhetoric. It is recommended that teachers alternate between a course in grammar one week and *Writing & Rhetoric: Chreia & Proverb* the next week. Another possibility would be to blend grammar into the Writing & Rhetoric exercises. Lessons in grammar can be inserted before the "Writing Time" exercises or after the "Speak It" section. The weekly schedule includes four days so that you have the flexibility to spend more time on revision or to cover additional exercises.

Day One

1. The teacher models fluency by reading the text aloud while students follow along silently.

2. "Tell It Back" (Narration) and "Talk About It" should immediately follow the reading of the text, while the story is still fresh in the students' minds. "Talk About It" is designed to help students analyze the meaning of texts and to see analogous situations, both in the world and in their own lives. Narration, the process of "telling back," can be done in pairs or by selecting individuals to narrate to the entire class. Playacting the story from memory is another possible form of narration. (Note: Solo students can tell back the story into a recording device or to an instructor.) The process of narration is intended to improve comprehension and long-term memory.

Day Two

1. Optional: The teacher can appoint a student or pair students to read the text again.

2. Students work with the text through the "Go Deeper" and "Writing Time" exercises. "Go Deeper" is all about building vocabulary and understanding the nuances of the text better. "Writing Time" includes dictation, sentence play, copiousness, and the chreia exercise itself. You may want more than one day for this step.

Day Three or Four*

1. A time of sharing work can wrap up each lesson. In order to build confidence and ability in public speaking, students should be encouraged to read their work aloud—either in pairs or to the entire class (or cohort).

2. The "Speak It" section creates opportunities for students to recite, to playact, and to share their work aloud. Please consider using a recording device whenever it would suit the situation. In this case, have the student listen to her recording to get an idea of what sounded right and what could be improved. Have students read the elocution instructions at the end of the book to help them work on skill in presentation.

3. At this level, teachers should give feedback to students and request rewrites whenever feasible. The art of writing is rewriting. Most students do not self-edit well at this age or provide useful feedback to each other. As the child gets older, self-editing checklists will be provided within the Writing & Rhetoric course.

---

*The number of days per week assigned to the lessons is four so that you have some flexibility according to the pace and level of depth that you can take advantage of with your students.

Introduction to Students

Here We Go Again

Clear your desks! Sharpen your pencils! We're back in action! If you've been blowing bubbles with your bubble gum, now's the time to knock it off! We don't want a big explosion to leave you with your eyelashes glued shut.

At this point you have most likely studied three Writing & Rhetoric books: *Fable*, *Narrative I*, and *Narrative II*. This next book will change things up a bit. You will still be enjoying stories about real people who lived in history: kings and queens, monks, brave women, and more. You will continue to read about their deeds and some of the wise things that they said. But here's the change: You will use these stories as background information for writing six-paragraph essays.

"Whoa!" you might say, "Get outta town! Six-paragraph essays? That sounds like a leap!" Well, yes, it is a bit of a leap, but this leap will come naturally to you. You will start with what you know and take it from there. In fact, you will be surprised by how capably you have been prepared by the previous books to write an essay.

In addition, the lessons in this book will give you a little help. Sometimes students are asked to conjure up essays from thin air. "Write an essay about an important goal you have for your life." "Describe an experience that has impacted you significantly." "Write about a happy moment in history and why it was so happy." Writing like this can be fun, but we believe that the best writing skills are developed when you have many ideas, words, and examples with which to work, so in this book, you will have writer guides to help you reach your destination.

The ability to think clearly on paper, and to share your thoughts orally, are skills that you will use for the rest of your life. Most of all, we want you to enjoy learning and writing about people who lived many long years ago. Who knows? They might actually become friends of yours across the distance of years and miles. Tallyho and away we go!

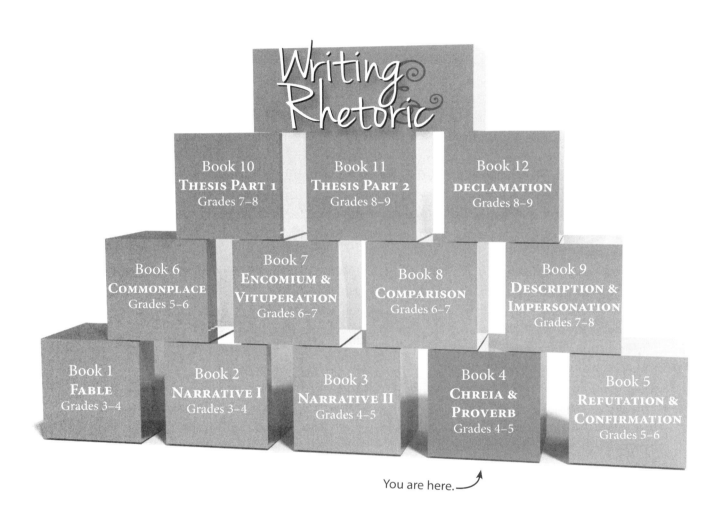

Writing & Rhetoric

Book 10
THESIS PART 1
Grades 7–8

Book 11
THESIS PART 2
Grades 8–9

Book 12
DECLAMATION
Grades 8–9

Book 6
COMMONPLACE
Grades 5–6

Book 7
ENCOMIUM & VITUPERATION
Grades 6–7

Book 8
COMPARISON
Grades 6–7

Book 9
DESCRIPTION & IMPERSONATION
Grades 7–8

Book 1
FABLE
Grades 3–4

Book 2
NARRATIVE I
Grades 3–4

Book 3
NARRATIVE II
Grades 4–5

Book 4
CHREIA & PROVERB
Grades 4–5

Book 5
REFUTATION & CONFIRMATION
Grades 5–6

You are here.

Introduction

Writing Happily

Where We Are Now with Writing

When it comes to writing, some students see the process as pure delight. That was my experience. I always loved taking a blank sheet of paper and transforming it into something magical: a carnival twinkling in the night, a city street shining with rain and reflecting gas lamps, an avalanche flying down a spire of rock. But I know that writing is not a magical world for many children or even some adults.

When I served as a writing instructor at the University of Southern California (USC), I saw first-hand the failure of writing instruction at our primary and secondary schools. Hardly a day went by that I wasn't grading a stack of papers, and the torment, the agony, of writing seemed to writhe through the pages.

Many of those college students had difficulty writing grammatically correct and coherent paragraphs—let alone entire essays, persuasively written. These were smart students from privileged backgrounds. So how did they get to college with such meager writing skills? What was happening in school or at home to sabotage the development of writing? Something was clearly not working.

Some years after teaching at USC, I helped to establish The Oaks Academy in the inner city of Indianapolis. Our school has grown from a modest 50 students in 1998 to 500-plus students today. At The Oaks, our mission is "to provide a rich, classical education to children of diverse racial and socioeconomic backgrounds." Our diversity includes children who grow up in highly involved families as well as children who have limited access to opportunity and must often fend for themselves academically.

As director of curriculum, I was determined to find a writing program that served the needs of all of our students. I wanted a program that combined the best modern practices with the principles of classical education as defined by such disparate educators as the Roman rhetorician Quintilian and nineteenth-century British reformer Charlotte Mason. I felt strongly that students could be confident, persuasive writers by the eighth grade if they received the right combination of models and practice. Above all, I wanted to avoid the wasted years that led to faltering communication in college and beyond.

I examined quite a few programs. Each in its own way seemed to be lacking—both the modern courses and those purporting to be classically inspired. Nothing seemed to be "just right." Some programs were difficult to use. Others seemed too frivolous on the one hand or too heavy on the other. Still others lacked the necessary incremental steps.

The book you have in your hand is the fruit of my dissatisfaction. This is a curriculum built on the solid foundations of the past and framed with the vitality of the present. This is a curriculum that has been tested by ancient, medieval, and modern kids and has proven reliable for the ages. Along with caring teachers and a diet of good books, the Writing & Rhetoric series has taken the young people of The Oaks, kids from all sorts of advantaged and disadvantaged backgrounds, and shaped them into fine communicators. As an eighth-grade teacher, I am often delighted by the rhetorical firepower in my classroom.

Imitation as a Foundation for Learning Writing

An examination of the theory and practice of modern composition reveals some obvious problems. Too often students are asked to brainstorm, "prewrite," or "free write" according to their personal interests. This means, in essence, that they are supposed to conjure ideas out of thin air. When faced with a blank piece of paper, many students naturally draw a blank. They lack a conversation in their heads about where to begin. Good writing requires content. It abhors a vacuum.

Students are also expected to write with no clear model before them. Modern composition scolds traditional writing instruction as rote and unimaginative. It takes imitation to task for a lack of freedom and personal expression. And yet effective communication from writer to reader always requires some sort of form and structure. Many of history's greatest writers learned by imitation. Benjamin Franklin, for example, taught himself to write by studying classic books and copying whole passages verbatim. He would then put the book aside and try to reconstruct the passage from memory.

Today's emphasis on originality and creativity has failed. When students lack a form by which to express their ideas, their creativity lacks vitality. As Alexander Pope tells us in his "An Essay on Criticism": "True Ease in Writing comes from Art, not Chance, / As those move easiest who have learn'd to dance." In other words, writing takes the same kind of determined study as ballet or diving. Creativity uses conventional form as a stage or a springboard from which to launch grand *jetés* and somersaults.

But there's yet another problem. Too often students are expected to tackle complex writing assignments without learning the necessary intermediate steps. Without the requisite scaffolding, teachers require summer vacation narratives, persuasive letters, research papers, and poetic descriptions. All of these forms require skills that must be developed in stages. It's too often assumed that everyone should be able to write well simply because most everyone can speak English well enough to be understood and form letters with a pencil. And yet how many of us would expect a child to sit at a piano, without piano lessons, and play a concerto? How many of us would expect a child with a hammer and a chisel and a block of marble to carve the statue of David as well as Michelangelo?

Writing is never automatic. The skills of the trade will not miraculously materialize somewhere along the school way. They take years to master. This is because writing demands thoughtfulness, organization, grammatical skill, rhetorical skill, and an ear for the English language. Most children have a natural inclination for one or two of these skills. Rarely do they have a knack for all. The other skills need to be developed and matured.

When it comes down to it, writing is simply thinking on paper (or thinking in some digital realm). Writing is thought translated to symbols—the symbolic language of the alphabet. The difficulty lies in the process of translation. I may picture a face or a waterfall clearly in my mind. It's quite another thing to describe the face or waterfall articulately in writing. I may have beautiful arguments on the tip of my tongue for buying a Great Dane puppy, but can I make the case persuasively on a piece of paper? The thinking comes first; the writing comes second. Both need to mature together.

What Is to Be Done

If we have lost our way, it rarely helps to plunge blindly forward. It often helps to retrace our steps. And so it is with writing. We have much to learn from the wisdom of the ages. The Greeks developed a system of persuasive speaking known as rhetoric. The Romans, who came later, were also in love with rhetoric, but they took it to the next level. In order to prepare their young students for dazzling oration, the Romans invented a complementary system of persuasive writing.

This writing system was so dynamic, so effective, that it outlasted the Roman Empire, the Middle Ages, and the Renaissance. It even survived into early modern times. This method employed fluent reading, careful listening, models for imitation, and progressive steps. In short, it did many of the things that are out of fashion today, but gave us writers such as Cicero and John Milton.

The Romans in the Greek-speaking part of the Empire called their system the *progymnasmata* (pro-gym-naz-ma-ta). This strange mouthful of a word derives from the same root for exercise as do "gymnasium" and "gymnastics." It means "preliminary exercises." The goal of these lessons is to prepare students for rhetoric, which is the art of writing well and speaking persuasively. This method assumes that students learn best by reading excellent examples of literature and by growing their skills through imitation. Successful writers study great writing. Successful orators study great speeches.

Each exercise is intended to impart a skill (or tool) that can be employed in all kinds of writing and speaking. The exercises are arranged from simple to more complex. What's more, the exercises are cumulative, meaning that later exercises incorporate the skills acquired in preceding exercises. This means, for example, that the skill of reporting or narrating (derived from the narrative exercise) will be regularly practiced and used in future exercises. While engaged in praising an individual (encomium exercise), a student will need to report or narrate an important event or achievement. While comparing two individuals (comparison exercise), a student will often need to praise one of those individuals (encomium).

Studying and acquiring the skills imparted by the *progymnasmata* (hereafter abbreviated *progym*) exercises is much like the way in which we acquire skill in cooking or in a sport such as soccer. In the case of cooking, students must first learn the foundational skills of measuring, pouring, and mixing. Then they must learn skills relating to using a frying pan and oven. Each recipe requires the employment of these foundational skills—no matter how complicated it is. A sport such as soccer also requires the mastery of basic skills such as kicking, passing, and dribbling. These foundational skills are carried forward into every soccer play and every game strategy.

Think of the *progym* as a step-by-step apprenticeship in the art of writing and rhetoric. What is an apprentice? It is a young person who is learning a skill from a master teacher. Our students will serve as apprentices to the great writers and great stories of history.

Quintilian, one of the master teachers of Rome, tells us that good habits are the foundation of education. In his *Institutio Oratoria*, he writes, "Once a bad habit has become ingrained, it is easier to break than bend. So strong is custom formed in early years." This master teacher also tells us that natural ability is nothing if it is not "cultivated by skillful teaching, persistent study, and continuous and extensive practice in writing, reading, and speaking."

Getting Started

The place to begin is reading, which should be encouraged as one of life's great pleasures from a child's earliest days. Parents should introduce books to babies as soon as they can keep their eyes open. Babies love to hear the sound of their parents' voices. They love the feeling of snuggling in a parent's lap. They love bright books and pictures. Reading helps develop joint attention, which is necessary for any language acquisition. The more a child reads and is read to, the better the foundation for writing. And if a parent feels he or she has been negligent in reading, it's never too late to get started.

The necessary corollary is that we must limit screens: TV, the Internet, and video games should stay off as much as possible! Without realizing it, many parents sabotage the ability of their children to think by allowing an excess of these media. Researchers are telling us, in no uncertain terms, that an imbalance of electronics can be harmful to clear thinking and focused attention. If children don't have time for books, they don't have time for glowing screens. (Unless, of course, that glowing screen contains a book.) Even boredom and daydreaming can be more productive than too much media exposure! A brain needs rest in order to do the hard work of synthesizing information, problem solving, and making connections between ideas.

Next to reading, it's important for children to get comfortable with the formation of letters. Children should work on penmanship to strengthen neural pathways that allow thinking and writing at the same time. Once writing mechanics come easily, it is much easier to make progress in the complex skill of "thinking on paper." As is often the case, there's more to a fine motor skill than meets the eye. With writing, children must learn to grip the pencil properly, to move their arms and wrists smoothly, and to stay focused on the page. Keep practice sessions short, but frequent.

Before children begin *Writing & Rhetoric: Chreia & Proverb* they should have covered the concepts in the previous three books. Many teachers and parents have begun older students with the *Fable*, *Narrative I*, and *Narrative II* books and worked through them to gain the skills those books offer.

After This—Formal Rhetoric

The formal study of rhetoric will develop in students a solid theoretical understanding of rhetoric, helping them to better understand why and how to employ the skills they have acquired while studying these exercises. The Writing & Rhetoric series (twelve books in all) will prepare students to enjoy transforming that blank sheet of paper into a spectacular view from atop the pinnacle of their own imagination.

Best Foot Forward

The *Progym* and the Practice of Modern Writing

Although the *progym* are an ancient method of approaching writing, they are extraordinarily relevant today. This is because modern composition owes almost everything to the *progym*. Modern writing borrows heavily from many of the *progym*'s various exercises. For example, modern stories are essentially unchanged from the ancient fable and narrative forms. Modern expository essays contain elements from the ancient chreia, the refutation/confirmation, and other *progym* exercises. Persuasive essays of today are basically the same as the ancient commonplace and thesis exercises. In this series, you can expect your students to grow in all forms of modern composition—narrative, expository, descriptive, and persuasive—while at the same time developing unique rhetorical muscle.

The *progym* cover many elements of a standard English and Language Arts curriculum. In *Chreia & Proverb* these include:

- writing informative/explanatory texts to examine a topic and convey ideas and information clearly
- introducing a topic or text clearly, stating an opinion, and creating an organizational structure in which related ideas are grouped to support the writer's purpose
- providing reasons that are supported by facts and details
- providing a concluding statement or section related to the opinion presented
- asking and answering questions to demonstrate understanding of the text
- summarizing the text
- producing clear and coherent writing in which the development and organization are appropriate to task, purpose, and audience
- drawing evidence from literary or informational texts to support analysis, reflection, and research.

While these goals are certainly worthwhile, the *progym* derive their strength from the incremental and thorough development of each form of writing. The Writing & Rhetoric series does not skip from form to form and leave the others behind, but rather builds a solid foundation of mastery by blending the forms. For example, no expository essay can truly be effective without description. No persuasive essay can be convincing without narrative. All good narrative writing requires description, and all good persuasive writing requires expository elements. Not only do the *progym* demand strong organization, but they retain all of the power of classical rhetoric.

Here is how the *progym* develop each stage of modern composition:

1. Fable—Narrative
2. Narrative—Narrative with descriptive elements
3. Chreia & Proverb—Expository essay with narrative, descriptive, and persuasive elements
4. Refutation & Confirmation—Persuasive essay with narrative, descriptive, and expository elements
5. Commonplace—Persuasive essay with narrative, descriptive, and expository elements
6. Encomium & Vituperation—Persuasive essay with narrative, descriptive, and expository elements
7. Comparison—Comparative essay with narrative, descriptive, and expository elements
8. Description & Impersonation—Descriptive essays with narrative, expository, persuasive, and comparative elements
9. Thesis Part 1—Persuasive essay with narrative, descriptive, expository, and comparative elements
10. Thesis Part 2—Persuasive speech with narrative, descriptive, expository, and comparative elements, as well as the three rhetorical appeals
11. Declamation—Persuasive essay or speech that marshals all the elements of the *progym* and brings them to bear upon judicial matters

As you can see, the *progym* move quickly to establish the importance of one form to another.

Objectives for *Chreia & Proverb*

Here are some of the major objectives for the exercises found in each section of this book:
1. Expose students to various proverbs, pithy sayings, and life stories, especially from the Middle Ages, and challenge the notion that this period of history was unrelentingly dark and morally ignorant.
2. Develop students' appreciation for the usefulness of concise sayings and actions and how these ideas impact their lives. To demonstrate that ideas and words influence actions.
3. Introduce students to the expository essay using a six-step outline. The predetermined outline helps students to organize their thinking into patterns of ideas.
4. Give students opportunities to creatively imitate and reshape proverbs and sayings.
5. Develop the concept of biographical narrative.
6. Introduce the idea of paraphrase as well as comparing and contrasting.
7. Model fluent reading for students and give them practice reading short texts.
8. Strengthen working memory through dictation, thus improving storage and manipulation of information.
9. Increase understanding of the flexibility and copiousness of language through sentence manipulation.
10. Facilitate student interaction with well-written texts through questions and discussion.

Lesson 1

What in the World Is a Chreia?

"**W**hoever loves discipline loves knowledge, but he who hates correction is stupid."[1] "A gentle answer turns away wrath, but a harsh word stirs up anger."[2] "Pride goes before destruction, a haughty spirit before a fall."[3]

Do you recognize these proverbs? They are said to have been composed by Solomon, a king of Israel, about three thousand years ago. A **proverb** is a wise saying or a short, clever insight into human behavior.

Because Solomon's proverbs are useful for teaching right and wrong, they all qualify as subjects for a ***chreia*** (cray-uh). The word "chreia" comes from the Greek word ***chreiodes*** (cray-o-dees), which means "useful." It is a short essay or remembrance that praises the author of a saying and shows why the saying is useful. If you were to say, "Let's hear it for Solomon, king of Israel, for the very useful proverb, 'Pride goes before destruction'!", that would not be exactly a chreia, but you would be on the right track.

1. Proverbs 12:1
2. Proverbs 15:1
3. Proverbs 16:18

In order to better understand how to write a chreia, take a look at one of Benjamin Franklin's proverbs. In *Poor Richard's Almanac*, Franklin wrote, "Fish and visitors stink after three days." This is a proverb that warns visitors not to stay for too many days at another person's house so they don't risk becoming unwelcome.

▶ Why do you think a visitor might become unwelcome after three days? Can you guess?

The problem with visitors is that they aren't really part of your family. It's harder to relax when a friend—even a very close friend—is hanging around. You feel that you need to focus on your visitor, make her happy, and do the things she wants to do. That takes a good deal of effort. You also need to be on your best behavior. You don't want your parents to snap at you or your brothers or sisters because you are behaving badly in front of a guest. It can be stressful on the whole family to be so "perfect." Your house has to be neat and tidy so your guest feels relaxed. Another thing: A guest usually doesn't do any work around the house. He isn't expected to mow the lawn or take out the trash or prepare the food. A guest for a day or two or three is a wonderful thing. But after three days he can sometimes become a burden. In some countries long-term guests become a working part of the family, but in America we are not used to this and can tire of guests more quickly.

To be able to write a decent chreia, you will need to know something about the life of the person being praised. Before you start writing any chreia in this book, you will read a short **biography**. "Biography" is a lovely Latin word borrowed from the Greeks. It combines the prefix *bio*, meaning "life," and *graphy*, meaning "description of." So a biography is a description of someone's life.

To show the usefulness of Franklin's proverb, a chreia can be written as follows:

First, praise the person who has said or written the proverb. In this case, Benjamin Franklin was the speaker. The chreia should show how the speaker lived his or her life according to the principles in the proverb or saying. For example:

How clever and wise of Benjamin Franklin to say, "Fish and visitors stink after three days!" Franklin was a highly practical man, and he published this advice in *Poor Richard's Almanac*. As a frequent traveler himself, Franklin tried never to overstay his welcome, even when he was ambassador to the courts of France, because he knew that the United States needed many friends.

Second, give a new version of the saying. You will use your own words to form a new proverb or rephrase the saying to show that you understand it. For example:

This amusing proverb might be rewritten to say, "Any visitor who stays too long at the home of a friend risks becoming as welcome as a vomiting cat."

Third, write why this proverb was said. Give details to explain why it might be useful. For example:

At first, a guest is a wonderful thing. What a joy it is to catch up with old friends and what fun it is to make new ones! But the longer a guest stays, no matter how close a friend he is, the more the host feels that his private space is being invaded. To most people in America, a home is a highly personal and private place—a place to rest from the work and conflict of everyday life. It is difficult to live for very long with a houseguest in one's personal space. If the guest remains a guest, he is taking advantage of the host. A guest expects certain privileges but does not share the responsibilities of the household.

Fourth, introduce a contrast. Think of an example of someone in history or in a story who didn't follow such wise advice or who didn't pay attention to such a useful saying. You'll want to give your example in the form of a very short narrative or story. For example:

In Latin the term *persona non grata* means "an unwelcome person." One example of such a person is Menelaus, king of Sparta, who received Paris, a prince of Troy, as an honored guest in his palace. He threw the young man a huge feast and gave him the freedom to wander his gardens. And how did Paris repay such fine hospitality? By flattering Menelaus's wife, Helen, and stealing her away. It was Paris's abduction of Helen that started the Trojan War. If there was ever a bad guest, a *persona non grata*, Paris certainly deserved the name.

Fifth, introduce a comparison. Now you'll want to think of an example of someone in history or in a story who lived by the wisdom of the saying. Again, give your example in the form of a very short narrative or story. For example:

> On the other hand, the poet Homer was always a welcome guest wherever he wandered. Legend tells us that he was a blind minstrel, little more than a beggar, but that he was in great demand for his skill as a storyteller. Greek chieftains and kings would throw feasts for Homer just to have him strum his harp and sing about the lives of two heroes, Achilles and Odysseus. His stories were so wonderful that they are still remembered today as the *Iliad* and the *Odyssey*.

Sixth, conclude with a brief epilogue. An epilogue is nothing more than a tidy ending for your essay. It is like the ribbon on a present that wraps up everything neatly. You can use a story from your own life as an example or conclude with any relevant thoughts. For example:

> I apply the "rule of three days" to myself whenever I am visiting friends. I try never to intrude on anyone's home for more than three days, unless I am particularly well acquainted with the family. Even then, I work to be as helpful as possible by washing the dishes and making my bed and helping to prepare the food for our meals. I would not want any of my acquaintances to think of dead fish when I enter their homes!

Does writing a chreia sound difficult? Never fear! This book will walk you through each stage of writing the essay. You'll see that it's not as complicated as it sounds. And as you get started, remember this very useful proverb: Nothing ventured, nothing gained.

Now take a look at the whole chreia put together:

> How clever and wise of Benjamin Franklin to say, "Fish and visitors stink after three days!" Franklin was a highly practical man, and he published this advice in *Poor Richard's Almanac*. As a frequent traveler himself, Franklin tried never to overstay his welcome, even when he was an ambassador to the courts of France, because he knew that the United States needed many friends.

This amusing proverb might be rewritten to say, "Any visitor who stays too long at the home of a friend risks becoming as welcome as a vomiting cat."

At first, a guest is a wonderful thing. What a joy it is to catch up with old friends and what fun it is to make new ones! But the longer a guest stays, no matter how close a friend he is, the more the host feels that his private space is being invaded. To most people in America, a home is a highly personal and private place—a place to rest from the work and conflict of everyday life. It is difficult to live for very long with a houseguest in one's personal space. If the guest remains a guest, he is taking advantage of the host. A guest expects certain privileges but does not share the responsibilities of the household.

In Latin the term *persona non grata* means "an unwelcome person." One example of such a person is Menelaus, king of Sparta, who received Paris, a prince of Troy, as an honored guest in his palace. He threw the young man a huge feast and gave him the freedom to wander his gardens. And how did Paris repay such fine hospitality? By flattering Menelaus's wife, Helen, and stealing her away. It was Paris's abduction of Helen that started the Trojan War. If there was ever a bad guest, a *persona non grata*, Paris certainly deserved the name.

On the other hand, the poet Homer was always a welcome guest wherever he wandered. Legend tells us that he was a blind minstrel, little more than a beggar, but that he was in great demand for his skill as a storyteller. Greek chieftains and kings would throw feasts for Homer just to have him strum his harp and sing about the lives of two heroes, Achilles and Odysseus. His stories were so wonderful that they are still remembered today as the *Iliad* and the *Odyssey*.

I apply the "rule of three days" to myself whenever I am visiting friends. I try never to intrude on anyone's home for more than three days, unless I am particularly well acquainted with the family. Even then, I work to be as helpful as possible by washing the dishes and making my bed and helping to prepare the food for our meals. I would not want any of my acquaintances to think of dead fish when I enter their homes!

Tell It Back—Narration

Without looking at the chreia in this lesson, tell back the most important information from it as best as you can remember it.

- What was the proverb?
- Who said it?
- Why is it useful?
- Who was the example of a bad guest and why?
- Who was the example of a good guest and why?
- How did the author bring the parts of the chreia together at the end?

Talk About It—

1. Have you ever stayed at someone's house for an extended period of time? Did your visit get better, get worse, or remain the same the longer you stayed?

2. Hospitality is important in every culture around the world. In Roman times, dusty travelers were often bathed, given fresh clothes, and entertained by dancing or song. During medieval times, a feast was thrown for noble travelers, and their horses were groomed and fed by stable boys. Monasteries gave every visitor, rich or poor, food and a bed for the night. In Arabia and India today, a big meal is served to guests, and guests must have the good manners to try every dish and eat to excess. What are some customs of hospitality in your family? How are guests treated in your home? Can you remember a very special time of hospitality in your life?

3. What makes a saying useful? Give examples of some useful sayings.

4. Is there a saying your mother or father often repeats?

Go Deeper—

For each question, circle or supply the correct answer(s).

1. What is a proverb?

   a. a verb that goes before a noun

   b. a very short story

   c. a wise saying

   d. a speech by King Solomon

2. What is the meaning of the Greek word *chreiodes*?

   a. clever

   b. useful

   c. complaining

   d. beautiful

3. What is a chreia?

   a. a short story with a moral

   b. a long essay about a proverb

   c. a study of several important people

   d. a short essay about a person's useful saying

4. The word "hospitality" derives from the Latin word *hospes*, which means "guest." If a host is supposed to show good hospitality to his guests, what is the most likely definition for "hospitality"?

   a. kindness to guests

   b. rudeness to guests

   c. dinner for guests

   d. a bed for guests

5. Use the word "hospitality" in your own complete sentence. Make sure that your sentence hints at the meaning of the word. In other words, a reader should be able to guess at what "hospitality" means because of your sentence.

_____

_____

_____

_____

6. How do you think the word "hospital," meaning "a place for healing the sick," is related to the word "hospitality"? In other words, what do a hospital and hospitality have in common?

_____

_____

_____

_____

7. In the following list, underline the sayings that might be useful for teaching wisdom or for teaching right from wrong.

   a. Go on up, you baldhead!
   b. Bend the tree while it is young.
   c. Early to bed, early to rise, makes a man healthy, wealthy, and wise.
   d. A horse! A horse! My kingdom for a horse!
   e. A rose is a rose is a rose.
   f. Do cats eat bats? Do bats eat cats?
   g. A living dog is better than a dead lion.

h. The love of money is the root of all kinds of evil.

i. No man can serve two masters.

j. I float like a butterfly, sting like a bee.

k. I came, I saw, I conquered. (*Veni, vidi, vici.*)

l. Be like a snail in planning and like a bird in getting things done.

m. Time is the wisest of all counselors.

n. Nonsense makes good sense.

Writing Time—

1. **DICTATION**—Your teacher will read a little part of the chreia from this lesson back to you. Please listen carefully! After your teacher reads once, she will read slowly again and include the punctuation marks. Your task will be to write down the sentence as your teacher reads it.

_____

_____

_____

_____

_____

2. **SENTENCE PLAY**—How clever and wise of Benjamin Franklin to say, "Fish and visitors stink after three days!" Use this sentence as a model to create similar sentences for the following sayings. Feel free to use different adjectives than "clever" and "wise." Remember that an adjective describes a noun.

Example: John Heywood said, "Look before you leap."
Change to: How smart and sensible of John Heywood to say, "Look before you leap!"

a. John Heywood said, "Two heads are better than one."

_____

_____

_____

b. Baltasar Gracian said, "A beautiful woman should break her mirror early."

_____

_____

_____

c. Jennifer Lynn said, "Some men are only handsome until they open their mouths."

_____

_____

_____

3. **COPIOUSNESS**—

A. If you'll recall, a synonym is a word that has nearly the same meaning as another word. Use synonyms to change the underlined nouns in Benjamin Franklin's proverb. Use specific species names for "fish." Following the example, write two new sentences that are roughly synonymous. Use a thesaurus only if you get stuck.

Example: <u>Fish</u> and <u>visitors</u> stink after three days.
Change to: Tuna and guests smell awful after three days.

i. _____

_____

_____

ii. _____

_____

_____

B. Add an adjective to describe both "fish" and "visitors." Add an adverb to describe the verb "stink." An adverb answers questions such as, "How?" "When?" and "Where?" and can describe verbs as well as adjectives and other adverbs.

Example: <u>Fish</u> and <u>visitors</u> <u>stink</u> after three days.
Change to: Dead fish and strange visitors stink terribly after three days.
In this sample sentence, "terribly" is the adverb. It describes how fish and visitors stink.

Example: <u>Fish</u> and <u>visitors</u> <u>stink</u> after three days.
Change to: Greasy fish and silly visitors stink frightfully after three days.
In this sample sentence, "frightfully" is the adverb. Again, it describes how fish and visitors stink.

i. _____

_____

_____

ii. _____

_____

_____

iii. _____

_____

_____

C. Use an adverb to replace the phrase "after three days." Change the tense of the verb as necessary. Your adverb should explain when, how, or where the fish will stink.

Example: Fish and visitors stink after three days.
Change to: Fish and visitors will stink tomorrow.
Change to: Fish and visitors always stink.
Some other adverbs you can use are "never," "often," "rarely," "sometimes," "soon," "yesterday," or "later."

i. _____

_____

_____

ii. _____

_____

_____

D. Move the prepositional phrase "after three days" to the beginning of the sentence. Now replace the phrase with a different prepositional phrase. Prepositions are often short words that show a time or space connection between words, such as "on," "around," "between," "near," "at," "by," "in," "out," "over," "under," "during," "since," and so on. A prepositional phrase begins with a preposition, such as "against all odds" and "down by the bank." In these sentences the prepositional phrase describes the conditions under which the fish and visitors will begin to stink.

Example: After three days, fish and visitors stink.
Change to: During hot weather, fish and visitors stink.
Change to: In the month of July, fish and visitors stink.

i. _____

_____

ii. _____

_____

4. **FABLE**—Do you remember fables from *Writing & Rhetoric: Fable*? Fables are short stories with a moral lesson, often with talking animals. Many proverbs serve as moral lessons for fables. "Slow and steady wins the race" is the moral lesson for *The Tortoise and the Hare*. "It is wise to learn from the misfortunes of others" is the moral lesson for *The Sick Lion*, in which a sickly Lion eats his guests. And the proverb "Self-conceit may lead to self-destruction" is the moral lesson for *The Frog and the Ox*.

Your job in this exercise is to take Benjamin Franklin's proverb "Fish and visitors stink after three days" and write a short fable to illustrate it as a moral lesson. Use animals that act like people to show how a guest becomes obnoxious to her host over the span of three days. How are things on the first day, the second day, the third day, and finally on the fourth day?

_____

_____

_____

_____

_____

_____

_____

_____

_____

_____

_____

_____

_____

_____

_____

_____

_____

_____

_____

_____

5. **THE FIVE *W*S PARAGRAPH**—Mothers and fathers give their kids lots of useful advice, even if a child doesn't want to hear it. Some of the things my parents told me included: "Eat your vegetables," "Wear a coat outside or you'll catch your death of cold," "If you're bored, clean your room," "Take a bath. A little soap and water never killed anybody," "You can't start the day on an empty stomach," and "Close the door. You weren't born in a barn!"

Write a short paragraph about a saying that your mother or father uses and discuss why it is useful. Remember to answer the five *W*s—who, what, when, where, why—and the one *H*—how. Who says the saying? What is the saying? When and where is the saying most often used? Why is the saying used? How do you feel about it? Use first-person point of view (using "I," "me," and "my"), as if you, the storyteller, are the main character of the story.

_____

_____

_____

_____

_____

_____

_____

_____

_____

_____

_____

_____

6. **POINT OF VIEW**—Rewrite the same short paragraph that you wrote in the last exercise, but use the third-person point of view only (using "he," "she," "it," "they," "him," "her," "it," "them," "his," "her," "its," "their"), as if the story's main character is someone other than you. Don't use the pronoun "I" at all, even though you are talking about your own family and experience. For example, you could start your paragraph by saying, "A mother frequently tells her daughter . . ." Be sure to answer the five *W*s and one *H*.

_____

_____

_____

_____

_____

_____

_____

_____

_____

_____

_____

_____

_____

_____

_____

_____

Speak It—

In this lesson you have studied Benjamin Franklin's saying about guests and hospitality. Research and narrate one of the stories in the following list, or use the sample story that follows. Then explain to your class what rules of hospitality were broken, either by the host or by the guest. Explain why these rules are important.

- *Abraham and the Three Visitors*, Genesis 18 in the Hebrew Scriptures
- *Ali Baba and the Forty Thieves*, Arabia
- *Beauty and the Beast*, France
- *Goldilocks and the Three Bears*, England
- *Hansel and Gretel*, Germany

- *Jack and the Beanstalk*, England
- *Jesus Anointed by a Sinful Woman*, Luke 7 in the Christian Scriptures
- *Odysseus and the Cyclops*, ancient Greece
- *Penelope and the Suitors*, ancient Greece
- *The Princess and the Pea*, Hans Christian Andersen
- *Vasilisa the Beautiful and Baba Yaga*, Russia.

Eat, My Coat, Eat

—adaptation of a Turkish tale by trickster Nasreddin Hodja

The Hodja was invited to a dinner party. Not wanting to be a show-off, the Hodja wore simple clothes. But when he got to the party, he found that everybody was dressed in their finest clothing and bedecked with jewels. These other people ignored him because they didn't want to be seen talking to someone in such plain clothing. They didn't even give him any food to eat. So the Hodja ran back home and put on his best suit and shoes. When he returned to the party, everybody greeted him warmly and invited him to sit down and eat.

When the soup was served, the Hodja dipped his sleeve into the bowl and said, "Eat, my coat, eat!" Everybody was shocked by this behavior. Then the Hodja took some meat and potatoes and stuffed them into his pockets. "Eat, my coat, eat!" he said.

Finally, the host asked the Hodja, "What's the matter with you? What are you doing?"

The Hodja replied, "When I first arrived here wearing my plain clothes, no one offered me anything to eat or drink. But now that I've come back wearing this fine coat, I was immediately offered the best of everything. I can only assume that it was the coat and not myself who was invited to your dinner party. So now I am feeding it."

_____

_____

_____

_____

_____

_____

_____

_____

_____

_____

_____

_____

_____

_____

_____

_____

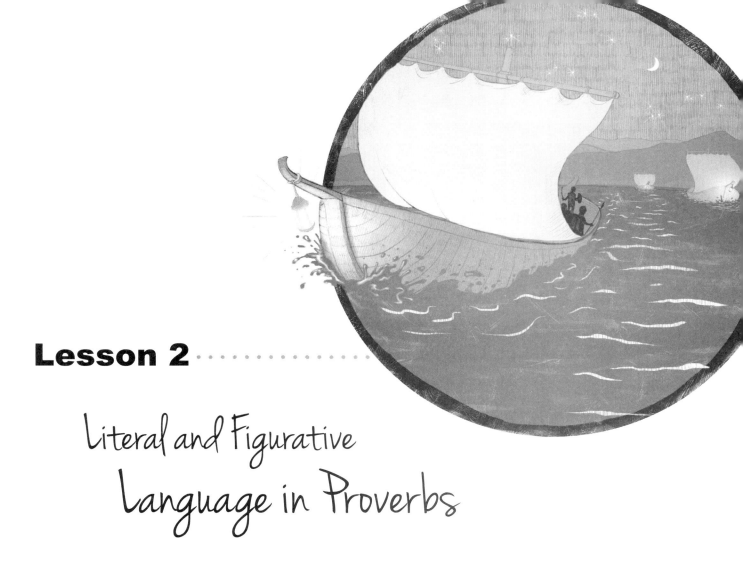

Lesson 2

Literal and Figurative Language in Proverbs

Many strokes **overthrow** the tallest oaks.

This proverb was written by John Lyly, an English playwright who came before William Shakespeare. It is certainly true that many strokes of an ax can chop down a big tree, which is the proverb's **literal** meaning, or the ordinary or factual meaning. But, as with all proverbs, this saying means more than its literal meaning.

▶ What else do you think the proverb can mean?

John Lyly has employed **figurative language** in this proverb. Figurative language is wording that suggests an imaginative meaning that goes beyond what the actual words say.

Say you're a great speller, but you lose the spelling bee. After the tournament, your teacher gives you a pat on the back and says, "That's the way the ball bounces." She's not talking about a literal ball. However, balls do bounce in unpredictable ways, and spelling bees take unpredictable turns. So your teacher is really saying, "Never mind. Don't worry about it. That's the way life goes sometimes." There are other ways of saying, "That's the way the ball bounces," or to emphasize the unpredictability of our lives. These include: "That's the way the cookie crumbles," "That's the way the dice roll," or simply, "That's life." In French it would be "*C'est la vie.*"

Take a look at another example of figurative language: Say you want to have a chat with a friend. You could say, "Come over and we'll chew the fat." Do you really want to chew fat? No, but when cooked right, fat is the tastiest part of meat, which people like to chew for its flavor and then spit out once the flavor is gone. Fat was once considered a very pleasurable thing to chew. "Let's chew the fat" is a figurative way of saying, "Let's have a nice, long, juicy talk." Other ways of saying the same thing include "Let's shoot the breeze" and "Let's chew the cud."

When John Lyly said, "Many strokes overthrow the tallest oaks," he was talking about more than chopping down a tree. He meant that it's possible to overcome a big obstacle with persistence and willpower or to do a difficult thing piece by piece. For example, we can't learn to play the piano in one day, but we can improve little by little every day. We can practice our scales and later be able to play songs that use those scales. In the same way, if we want to change a bad habit, which rarely goes away all at once, we must work on it little by little. This is the figurative, or deeper, meaning beneath the literal illustration of a person chopping down a tall tree with one ax swing after another.

There are other sayings that use figurative language to show the importance of persistence. Here are a few:
- The journey of a thousand miles begins with a single step.
- Drips of water may wear down a great stone.
- Pebble by pebble, an ant may raise a mountain.

Now take a look at a different proverb: "Let sleeping dogs lie." What is the literal meaning of this saying? Obviously, it is that if you see a dog, you should let it keep sleeping. What is the deeper meaning of the figurative language? In other words, what lesson is this proverb trying to teach? If you wake up a sleeping dog, it could be in a snappish mood and bite you. Therefore, don't go looking for trouble.

Can you think of other figurative ways to express the idea of "Don't go looking for trouble"?

- If it isn't broken, don't try to fix it.
- Don't try to count the teeth of a crocodile.
- Give a roaring lion plenty of room.
- Swim like a fish, but not with the sharks.

Now it's time for you to sort out the figurative meanings of some proverbs and to write your own.

Talk About It—

1. There's a Nigerian proverb that says, "When elephants fight, it is the grass that suffers." What is the literal meaning of this proverb? What do you think is the deeper meaning of the figurative language? Hint: Think of the elephants as kings or powerful people.

2. The Chinese have a saying, "One mouse dropping ruins a whole pot of porridge." What is the literal meaning of this proverb? What do you think is the deeper meaning of the figurative language? Compare this proverb to the English proverb "One bad apple spoils the bunch."

3. The Indians have a saying, "Distant hills always look most beautiful." What is the literal meaning of this proverb? What do you think is the deeper meaning of the figurative language? Compare this proverb to the English proverb "The grass is always greener on the other side of the fence."

4. Why do you think people all over the world create proverbs? Why are they useful?

Go Deeper—

1. See if you can match the following proverbs with their deeper meanings. Put the correct letter in the space next to the proverb.

   _____ Don't bother giving ginger to a monkey. —India

   _____ When it rains, it pours. —England

   _____ Your elbow is close, but you can't bite it. —Russia

   _____ The cub is from the lion. —Africa

   A. The child is like the parent.
   B. Things are not as easy as they look.
   C. Don't waste valuable things on ungrateful people.
   D. Troubles never come alone.

2. The deeper meaning of a proverb is usually shared by many other proverbs. See if you can match the list of meanings from the previous exercise with proverbs from other parts of the world. Put the correct letter in the space next to the proverb.

   _____ The child is like the parent.

   _____ Things are not as easy as they look.

   _____ Don't waste valuable things on ungrateful people.

   _____ Troubles never come alone.

   A. Don't cast your pearls before the swine.
   B. Like father, like son. Like mother, like daughter.
   C. One stone causes an **avalanche**.
   D. It's one thing to hear a mosquito, another thing to kill it.

Writing Time—

1. **DICTATION**—Your teacher will read two proverbs to you. Please listen carefully! After your teacher reads once, she will read slowly again and include the punctuation marks. Your task will be to write down the sentences as your teacher reads them one by one.

_____

_____

_____

_____

2. **SENTENCE PLAY**—<u>Pebble by pebble, an ant may raise a mountain.</u> Follow this sentence pattern to create a new proverb about something small becoming something big, or about something difficult overcome by little steps.

   Examples: Grain by grain, a farmer feeds a nation.

             Footstep by footstep, we walk around the world.

   a. Drop by drop, _____

   _____.

   b. Push-up by push-up, _____

   _____.

   c. _____

   _____, a composer creates a symphony.

3. **COPIOUSNESS**—When writing, you'll mostly want to use active voice. In active voice, the subject of the sentence performs an action. Take this sentence, for example: "I lit the candle." In this case, the subject is "I." The action is lighting the candle. In the sentence "Oliver kicked the rhinoceros," Oliver is the subject. The action is kicking the rhinoceros.

Active voice uses strong verbs and is livelier and less wordy than passive voice. The passive voice uses weak verbs (such as "is," "am," "are," "was," "were," "be," "being," "been"), and the subject is not doing the action. Rather, some action is being done to the subject and the subject just seems to sit there doing absolutely nothing. Look at the same two sentences in passive voice: "The candle was lit by me" and "The rhinoceros was kicked by Oliver." Notice how the candle and the rhino are just sitting there while "me" and "Oliver" are doing the acting. Both passive-voice sentences aren't quite as zippy as the two sentences in active voice.

A. Change the following sentences from passive to active voice. Keep the same verb tense.

Example: The runner was cheered by the crowd.

Change to: The crowd cheered the runner.

i. The boat was rocked by the wave.

_____

_____

ii. Every Saturday, clean laundry is hung up by the maid.

_____

_____

iii. When it's bedtime, stories are read to me by Dad.

_____

_____

iv. The cavity in the patient's tooth will be drilled by the dentist.

_____

_____

v. Write your own sentence, using active voice, about a rhinoceros knocking down a tree.

_____

_____

Lesson 2: Literal and Figurative Language in Proverbs

B. This time, work the other way around. Change the sentences from active voice to passive voice. Keep the same verb tense.

Remember that you really don't want to use passive voice very often. You are doing this exercise so that you learn to recognize weak passive-voice sentences in your own writing.

Example: At the pizza parlor, Mom ordered two large pies.
Change to: At the pizza parlor, two large pies were ordered by Mom.

i. The cat will scratch the boy.

_____

_____

ii. Paco gave Maria a gift for her birthday.

_____

_____

iii. A thief must have broken the window.

_____

_____

iv. Li-Hua picks a basket of pears.

_____

_____

v. Write your own sentence using passive voice.

_____

_____

C. Some sentences fall flat because the writer uses a state-of-being verb when she could use an action verb instead. State-of-being verbs belong to the "to be" verb family; they are words such as "is," "am," "were," "was," "are," "be," "been," "being."

Lesson 2: Literal and Figurative Language in Proverbs

Which do you think is the more interesting sentence: "The cat is on my face," or "The cat sleeps on my face"? The verb "sleep" is more interesting than "is" because it paints a more vivid picture. How about this one: "The logs were bright," or "The logs flamed brightly"? Thanks to the second sentence, you know why the logs are bright: The logs are on fire. "Flamed" is a more interesting verb than "were."

In this next exercise, change the underlined state-of-being verbs into action verbs. You may alter the sentence as long as the meaning remains nearly the same.

Example: Hu is in China every summer.

Change to: Hu visits China every summer.

i. The wolf <u>was</u> in the forest, waiting for Little Red Riding Hood.

_____

_____

ii. Little Red carried a basket of shortbread cookies that <u>were</u> delicious.

_____

_____

iii. While she <u>was</u> in the dark trees, she noticed some bushes moving up ahead.

_____

_____

iv. The wolf <u>was</u> like a beast when he pounced, and he <u>was</u> happy to gobble the cookies.

_____

_____

v. Next time, Little Red <u>will be</u> with a basket of poison-ivy cupcakes.

_____

_____

D. <u>The medicine is worse than hot sauce.</u> Change this sentence two ways using an active verb. You may alter the sentence as long as the meaning remains nearly the same.

    i. _____

      _____

    ii. _____

      _____

4. **CREATE A NEW PROVERB**—Read through the following list of some common proverbs. For each one, first write the proverb's literal meaning. (Remember, the literal meaning is what the sentence is actually describing.) Then write the proverb's figurative meaning. (The figurative meaning illustrates a new idea that goes beyond what the actual words say.) Finally, write a new proverb using different language and images to suggest the proverb's figurative meaning.

Example 1: Don't count your chickens before they're hatched.
    i. Literal meaning: Not all eggs hatch, so don't imagine owning a whole flock of hens until they do.
    ii. Figurative meaning: Don't be so confident that you take success for granted.
    iii. New proverb: Don't cross the bridge before you come to the river, or Don't think you've won the game before you score a goal.

Example 2: Birds of a feather flock together.
    i. Literal meaning: Birds that look alike gather together in flocks.
    ii. Figurative meaning: People who act alike usually hang out together.
    iii. New proverb: If you're a thief, your friends will be thieves.

A. Look before you leap.

    i. Literal meaning: _____

      _____

ii. Figurative meaning: _____

_____

iii. New proverb: _____

_____

B. It was the straw that broke the camel's back.

   i. Literal meaning: _____

_____

   ii. Figurative meaning: _____

_____

   iii. New proverb: _____

_____

C. You can't tell a book by its cover.

   i. Literal meaning: _____

_____

   ii. Figurative meaning: _____

_____

   iii. New proverb: _____

_____

D. The burnt child dreads the fire.

   i. Literal meaning: _____

_____

   ii. Figurative meaning: _____

_____

iii. New proverb: _____

_____

E. Beggars can't be choosers.

   i. Literal meaning: _____

   _____

   ii. Figurative meaning: _____

   _____

   iii. New proverb: _____

   _____

5. **COMPARE PROVERBS**—Choose a set of proverbs from the following suggestions. Write a short paragraph comparing the two similar proverbs. In your paragraph, answer the following questions:

   ● What are the proverbs and what do they mean?

   ● Where (in what countries) are the proverbs used?

   ● Why and how are the proverbs useful?

   Example: One day of cold weather won't make three feet of ice. —China

   Rome was not built in a day. —France/Italy

   Paragraph:

   Two proverbs share a similar meaning. The first proverb, "One day of cold weather won't make three feet of ice," and the second proverb, "Rome was not built in a day," both mean "Big things can't be done quickly." Whenever we start a big job or begin a significant undertaking, it's important to know that it can't be rushed. If we understand the truth of these proverbs, we will be patient and give any task the time and effort it deserves.

A. If you breed crows, they will peck out your eyes. —Mexico

As you make your bed, so you must lie in it. —England

B. Talk does not cook rice. —China

Many words won't fill a bushel basket. —America

_____

_____

_____

_____

_____

_____

_____

_____

_____

_____

6. **CREATE YOUR OWN PROVERBS**—After reviewing the examples given, create your own proverbs using figurative language to express the ideas listed.

Examples:

Idea: A person who brags a lot lacks substance.

Proverb: Some people are all sizzle and no steak.

Idea: Be useful where you are.

Proverb: Bloom where you're planted.

A. Idea: Something may look good on the outside but be bad on the inside.

Proverb: _____

_____

B. Idea: As soon as something is born, it begins to die.

Proverb: _____

_____

C. Idea: No work gains no reward.

Proverb: _____

_____

D. Idea: Happiness comes from having a clear conscience.

Proverb: _____

_____

E. Idea: Weak people should stand together against a bully.

Proverb: _____

_____

Speak It—*Lexis* and Inflection

Say your friend jumps out of a closet and scares you. You warn him with the proverb, "What goes around, comes around!" That is not public speaking. Or say you're at a pool party and you shout, "Hey, everybody. Watch me do a cannonball!" That is not public speaking, either. Public speaking is speaking formally to a group of people, such as when you recite a poem to your class or give a speech to parents. It is something you practice ahead of time.

You already know that proper elocution, or the manner of presentation of a formal speech, is important for public speaking. Ancient educators taught us nearly everything we know about rhetoric, the practice of persuasive speaking. Aristotle noted two important parts of rhetoric: *logos* and *lexis*. *Logos* is Greek for "word" and also for "logical reasoning." So *logos* is the content, the substance of a speech. It's what you put down on paper and the words that are spoken. *Lexis* is the delivery of the words, how the speech comes across to the audience.

Both *logos* and *lexis* are important for effective public speaking. We might call them substance and style today. The content of a speech can mean the difference between sharing excellent ideas or spouting stuff and nonsense. The way you use your voice in speaking can mean the difference between catching the interest of your audience or putting it to sleep.

▶ Can you remember some important ways to improve the delivery, or *lexis*, of a speech?

You already know that proper volume—loudness and softness—is vital to *lexis*. Speed—how quickly or slowly you speak—is also key. In addition to proper volume and speed, there is also **inflection**. What is inflection?

Think about the different ways you could say the words, "I'd like to have you for dinner." If you say this sentence in a nice, casual voice, it sounds as if you are inviting someone to your house for a meal. If you say it sarcastically, it sounds like you really don't want her to come over for dinner. If you say it in a raspy, wolfish voice, it sounds as if you want to eat someone up. The change in the pitch or tone of your voice is called inflection.

Try to say the following proverbs with different inflections to give them different meanings:

- A big nose never spoils a handsome face.
- If you hang around dogs, you'll get fleas.

In order to hold your audience's attention, you are going to need to use the highs and lows of your voice. Inflection tells the audience when they need to be excited or when they should laugh or get serious. We know that when a person asks us a question, his voice will get a little higher at the end of his sentence. We know when we're about to hear bad news because a person's voice goes lower. A good speaker will know how to use inflection to make his speech more powerful.

Now try reading something longer with inflection. After you become acquainted with the content of the following passages, practice saying the passages using different inflections, speeds, and volumes. The passages are

Lesson 2: *Literal and Figurative Language in Proverbs*

adapted from John Haaren and A.B. Poland's *Famous Men of the Middle Ages* and from M.B. Synge's *The Discovery of New Worlds*.

1. Speak this passage by changing inflection, that is the pitch and tone of your voice. Speak it tragically, lightheartedly, and with no emotion.

> Now we come to a time when the power of Rome was broken. Tribes of barbarians who lived north of the Danube and Rhine Rivers took possession of lands that had been part of the Roman Empire. These tribes were the Goths, Vandals, Franks, and Anglo-Saxons. From them have come some of the greatest nations of modern times, including Germany, France, and England. All belonged to the same race and are known as Teutons, or Germans.
>
> Some thirteen years after the death of Constantine, a great change took place in the position of the Germans. Suddenly a horde of fierce fighters appeared from the wild regions of Central Asia. They were the terrible Huns, who had fought their way over the high tablelands of Asia until they reached the Sea of Azov and found the land of the Goths. On rolled the flood of invaders, striking terror before them, conquering the lands of the Goths, pressing ever on and on toward the Danube, the great Roman boundary.
>
> Dreading the fate that awaited them, the Goths looked across the broad Danube at Rome, with its well-tilled plains beyond, and at last they crossed over. Day after day and night after night ships crossed and re-crossed the Danube, until thousands of Gothic warriors with their wives and children stood on the soil of the Roman Empire, while the watchfires of the Huns blazed away behind them on the other side of the river.

2. After you have read it for content, speak this passage slowly, quickly, and moderately. Then vary the speed to make it sound best.

> The Teutonic tribes worshiped the same gods. Like the old Greeks and Romans, they had many gods.

Woden, who was also called Odin, was the greatest god of all. His name means "mighty warrior," and he was king of all the gods. He rode through the air mounted on Sleipnir, an eight-footed horse that was fleeter than an eagle. When the tempest roared, the Teutons said it was the snorting of Sleipnir. Our name for Wednesday comes from Woden—"Wednesday" meaning "Woden's day."

3. After you have read this passage and understand it, speak this passage loudly, softly, and somewhere in-between. Then vary the volume to make it sound best. Thor, a son of Woden, ranked next to Woden among the gods. He rode through the air in a chariot drawn by goats. The Germans called him Donar and Thunar, words which sound like "thunder." From this we can see that he was the thunder god. In his hand he carried a wonderful hammer, which always came back to his hand when he threw it. Its head was so bright that as it flew through the air it made lightning. When it struck the vast ice mountains they reeled and splintered into fragments, and thus Thor's hammer made thunder. Our name for Thursday comes from Thor—"Thursday" meaning "Thor's day."

4. Find the proverb in the story: When you are done practicing your elocution, see if you, with your class or parents, can figure out a proverb for the passage about the fall of Rome in #1 of this section. Be sure to share your proverb with the proper inflection.

Lesson 2: Literal and Figurative Language in Proverbs

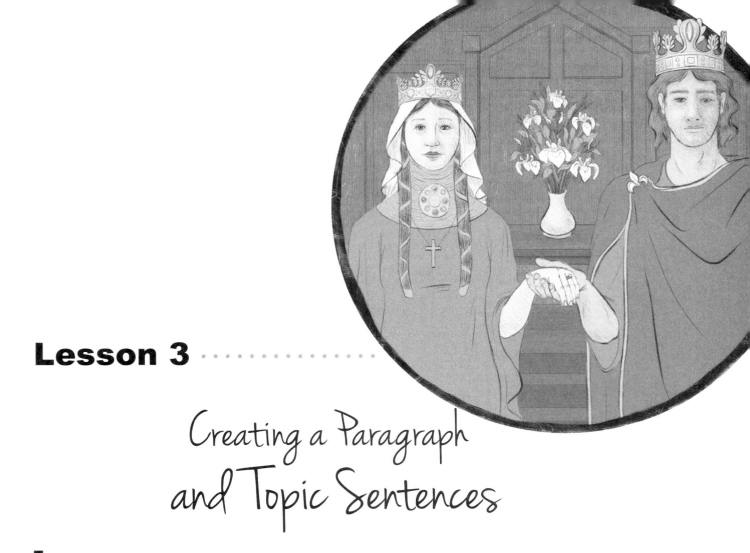

Lesson 3

Creating a Paragraph and Topic Sentences

I know that you are eager to dive headfirst into the chreia pool. You can't wait to start swimming around—I know, I know! Before you do, however, let's have a short lesson on creating **paragraphs**. It will make everything easier in the long run, and there will be less danger of drowning. I promise to be brief.

You'll notice that almost every book is divided up into paragraphs. Paragraphs are marked by indentations on the first line or by a space between each paragraph. If you don't believe me, pick up a book and see paragraphs in action.

▶ So what is a paragraph?

When you read the following passage, you'll see that it's all jumbled and very hard to understand:

> Knights fought on horseback, and the word "chivalry" comes from the French word *cheval*, meaning "a horse." Be courageous in battle. It was a lasting disgrace! They were to come to the rescue of any lady in distress or danger.

Chivalry was a code of behavior for knights. She would not marry a coward or a braggart, even if he owned ten thousand acres of land. In those rough days of the Middle Ages, beautiful ideas, in the form of chivalry, started to blossom. The worst thing a knight could do was to be rude to a lady. By the code of chivalry, knights learned to truly value women. Always treat people with good manners. They were to serve the lady and fight for her good name. Speak the truth instead of lies. Above all, never insult a lady. And she would never give her love to any man who was not worthy of her. Be gentle in peace.

Now see how much more sense these sentences make when they are organized into two tidy paragraphs and order is given to the material:

Chivalry was a code of behavior for knights. Knights fought on horseback, and the word "chivalry" comes from the French word *cheval*, meaning "a horse." In those rough days of the Middle Ages, beautiful ideas, in the form of chivalry, started to blossom. These were ideas such as: Be courageous in battle. Be gentle in peace. Always treat people with good manners. Speak the truth instead of lies. Above all, never insult a lady.

The worst thing a knight could do was to be rude to a lady. It was a lasting disgrace! By the code of chivalry, knights learned to truly value women. They were to come to the rescue of any lady in distress or danger. They were to serve the lady and fight for her good name. And she would never give her love to any man who was not worthy of her. She would not marry a coward or a braggart, even if he owned ten thousand acres of land.

Each of these paragraphs focuses on a single idea. The first paragraph seeks to define the word "chivalry." The second paragraph describes the most important aspect of chivalry: how knights treated ladies and how ladies treated knights.

The most important sentence in each paragraph is called the **topic sentence**. This is the sentence that tells what the paragraph is about. A topic sentence can come anywhere in a paragraph, but most often it appears at the beginning.

▶ Look at the two previous paragraphs and see if you can locate the topic sentence in each of them.

Think of a paragraph as a sailboat in a fleet of sailboats, all going in the same direction, all heading to the same destination. The topic sentence is like the rudder on each boat that helps to keep it on course.

Now take a few minutes to play with paragraphs and topic sentences so that these ideas truly sink into your noggin.

Tell It Back—Narration

- Without looking at the text, tell back the definitions of "paragraph" and "topic sentence," and describe why they are both important.

Go Deeper—

- Underline the topic sentence in each of the following paragraphs. Remember, the topic sentence tells us the main idea of the paragraph.

Food During the Middle Ages
—adapted from *Manners, Customs, and Dress During the Middle Ages and During the Renaissance Period* by Paul Lacroix

a. Pork was the most important meat during the Middle Ages. In those remote days, when the land was still covered with enormous forests of oak, much space was devoted to pigs, whose special liking for acorns is well known. Thus the bishops, princes, and lords caused many herds of pigs to be fed on their lands. There was no great feast at which hams, sausages, and black puddings were not served on all the tables.

b. Even in the city of Paris, there was scarcely a townsman who did not have two or three young pigs. There were so many pigs that they made a nuisance of themselves. During the day these unsightly creatures were allowed to roam in the streets. Pigs did keep the streets clean by eating up garbage of all sorts, which was thrown out of the houses, but they also left behind dung. One of the sons of Louis the Fat fell off his horse and fractured his skull after a pig ran between the horse's legs.

c. For many centuries fattened geese were more highly prized than any other kind of poultry. Charlemagne ordered that his domains should be well stocked with flocks of geese. Goose herders drove these tame geese to feed in the fields like flocks of sheep. These birds were considered a great delicacy by peasants and townspeople alike.

d. Desserts of the Middle Ages were different than those we have today. There was a dish, called "dessert," that was made with pears, crabapples, peeled walnuts, figs, dates, peaches, grapes, filberts, spices, and red sugar plums. After dinner, wealthy people also ate wafers with spiced wine. They enjoyed jellies molded in the shapes of swans, peacocks, and herons.

Writing Time—

1. **DICTATION**—Your teacher will read a quote from a paragraph at the beginning of this lesson. Please listen carefully! After your teacher reads once, she will read slowly again and include the punctuation marks. Your task will be to write down the sentences as your teacher reads them one by one.

_____

_____

_____

_____

_____

2. **SENTENCE PLAY**—There were so many pigs that they made a nuisance of themselves. During the day these unsightly creatures were allowed to roam in the streets. Notice how the second sentence flows smoothly from the topic sentence. The second sentence gives you information about why the pigs were such a nuisance.

Lesson 3: *Creating a Paragraph and Topic Sentences*

If you change the topic sentence, how would that change the sentence that comes next? In the following exercises, write a second sentence that flows from the first.

Example: <u>There were so many birds that they made people happy.</u> During the day these bright-feathered creatures sang songs so sweetly.

a. There were so many dogs that they made a nuisance of themselves.

_____

_____

_____

b. There were so many goldfish that they made people happy.

_____

_____

_____

3. **COPIOUSNESS**—Mark the correct part of speech for the underlined words in the following passage. Place an *N* over the nouns, an *ADJ* over the adjectives, and a *V* over the verb. Remember that a noun is a person, place, thing or idea, an adjective describes a noun, and a verb is often the action word of the sentence. Then rewrite the passage with synonyms for the underlined words.

In those <u>rough</u> days of the Middle Ages, <u>beautiful</u> ideas, in the form of

chivalry, <u>started</u> to blossom. These were ideas such as: Be <u>courageous</u>

in <u>battle</u>. Be <u>gentle</u> in peace. Always treat people with <u>good</u> <u>manners</u>.

Speak the truth instead of <u>lies</u>.

_____

_____

Lesson 3: *Creating a Paragraph and Topic Sentences*   39

_____

_____

_____

_____

_____

_____

_____

4. **PARAGRAPHS**—Divide the following narrative about the Frankish king Clovis into four paragraphs. Draw a line between sentences to show where a new paragraph should start. Remember that a paragraph is a group of well-organized sentences that form an idea.

 The four ideas are as follows:

a. The first paragraph talks about Clovis's youth and character.

b. The second paragraph introduces the problem of the Romans.

c. The third paragraph talks about the Battle of Soissons.

d. The fourth paragraph talks about Clotilde, the woman Clovis hopes to marry.

Clovis, the First French King

—adapted from *Famous Men of the Middle Ages* by John H. Haaren

Each tribe of the Franks had its own king. The greatest of all these kings was Clovis, who became ruler of his tribe in the year 481. Clovis was then only sixteen years of age. But though he was so young, he proved in a very short time that he could govern as well as older men. He was intelligent and brave. No one ever knew him to be afraid of anything, even when he was but a child. When Clovis became king of the Franks, a great part of Gaul still belonged to Rome. This part was then governed by a Roman general named Syagrius. Clovis resolved to drive the Romans out of the country, and he talked over the matter with the head men of his army. "My desire," said he, "is that the Franks shall have possession of every part of this fair land. I shall drive the Romans and their friends away and make Gaul the empire of the Franks." Near the city of Soissons, the Roman army met the Frankish army. The Romans thought that they would win the victory easily, but they were mistaken. Every time that they made a charge upon the Franks they were beaten back by the warriors of Clovis. The young king himself fought bravely at the head of his men and with his own sword struck down a number of the Romans. He tried to find Syagrius and fight with him, but the Roman commander was nowhere to be found. Early in the battle he had fled from the field, leaving his men to defend themselves as best they could. The Franks gained a great victory that day. Not very long after Clovis became king he heard of a beautiful young girl, the niece of Gondebaud, king of Burgundy, and he thought he would like to marry her. Her name was Clotilde, and she was an orphan, for her wicked uncle Gondebaud had killed her father and mother. Clovis sent one of his nobles to Gondebaud to ask to have her for his wife. At first Gondebaud thought of refusing to let the girl go. He feared that she might have him punished for the murder of her parents if she became the wife of so powerful a man as Clovis. But he was also afraid that by refusing he would provoke the anger of Clovis, so he permitted the girl to be taken to the court of the king of the Franks. Clovis was delighted when he saw her, and they were immediately married.

5. **TOPIC SENTENCE**—The following paragraphs are missing topic sentences. Read each paragraph to determine its subject, then write a topic sentence that would help the reader to better understand what the paragraph is about.

a. In the gate of a castle there were murder holes, through which hot oil or boiling water could be poured on the heads of attackers. There were arrow loops in the walls and towers. Archers could shoot out of these holes and hit anyone who dared to come too close. When attackers brought up rams to break down the doors, castle defenders threw heavy stones down on their heads.

   Write your topic sentence about castle defenses.

   _____

   _____

   _____

   _____

b. The churches are a blaze of lights. The markets are packed with pyramids of oranges, melons, and lemons. The shops are brilliantly illuminated and profusely decorated with ribbons and flowers. Bonfires are lighted; a great slaughter of turkeys is enacted, to the loud accompaniment of protests screeched by the flocks of birds awaiting their last moment; streets are thronged with an excited populace, diving in and out of shops, dancing on the pavements, processing along the roads, lingering to enjoy the sights.
   —from *Peeps At Many Lands: Spain* by Edith A. Browne

   Write your topic sentence about Christmas Eve in Spain.

   _____

   _____

   _____

   _____

c. When the silkworm is fully grown, it spins around itself a small ball of **silk** called a cocoon. If this cocoon were left to itself, the worm would change to a moth, and the moth would eat its way out of this little house. But this, of course, would cut the little threads and spoil the silk. Therefore, as soon as the cocoon is made, it is put into hot water to kill the worm. In this way the silk is saved. —from *Home Geography for Primary Grades* by C.C. Long

Write your topic sentence about where silk comes from.

_____

_____

_____

_____

Speak It—

If the topic sentence is the most important sentence in a paragraph, it should be emphasized in public speaking. Deliver the following paragraphs with proper elocution, but try speaking more softly or more loudly when you come to the underlined topic sentence. Your audience will listen more carefully when you use volume—loudness or softness—to emphasize a sentence.

Medieval Medicine

—adapted from *Medieval Medicine* by James J. Walsh

The first modern university formed around a medical school in Salerno, Italy. <u>There, medical monks encouraged good cleanliness as the way to good health.</u> They believed very much in early rising, washing in cold water, thorough cleansing, and exercise in the open air without sudden cooling afterwards. They even made up a rhyme to teach cleanliness:

At early dawn, when first from bed you rise,

Wash, in cold water, both your hands and eyes.

With brush and comb then cleanse your teeth and hair,

And thus refreshed, your limbs outstretch with care.

<u>The greatest surprise of the whole range of medical history is that medieval surgeons anticipated many medical advances.</u> Medieval surgeons washed wounds with wine, scrupulously removing every foreign particle. Then they brought the edges of the wound together, not allowing wine or anything else to remain within. Dry surfaces were their desire so that the skin could knit together. Upon the outer surface they laid only lint steeped in wine. They killed germs with wine long before germs were discovered.

<u>Medieval surgeons also wanted to operate painlessly on their patients.</u> Some surgeons prescribed drugs, such as opium, the juice of the morel, mandrake, ivy, hemlock, or lettuce, which sent the patient to sleep, so that the incision would not be felt. A new sponge was soaked in the juice of these items and left to dry in the sun; when the surgeons needed it, they put a sponge into warm water and then held it under the nostrils of the patient until he went to sleep. Then they performed the operation.

Lesson 3: *Creating a Paragraph and Topic Sentences*

Lesson 4

First Chreia— King Solomon

King Solomon of Israel

—adapted, in part, from *Hurlbut's Story of the Bible* by Jesse Lyman Hurlbut

As a door turns on its hinges, so a sluggard turns on his bed.

—Proverbs 26:14 (Solomon, circa 960–922 BC)

You may already know something about King Solomon of Israel, the famous maker of proverbs. The great work of Solomon's reign was the building of a massive temple for the worship of Yahweh (one name for God in the Hebrew Scriptures). This temple stood on Mount Moriah, on the east of Mount Zion, and it covered much of the mountain. King David, Solomon's father, had prepared for it by gathering great stores of gold, silver, stone, and cedar wood. The walls were made of stone, and the roof of cedar.

We learn from the Scriptures that when he was a young man, Solomon felt overwhelmed by the responsibility of ruling a kingdom (see 1 Kings 3:7-9). A king had to punish criminals and bring justice to their victims. He had to raise taxes and ensure that the money was spent on important projects such as wells for water and walls for defense. He had to supervise the construction of public buildings such as temples and palaces. With neighboring countries, he had to be a good diplomat and seek to win their friendship. When enemies threatened the borders of Israel, the king was compelled to lead his soldiers into battle. He always had to protect his kingdom from rebellion and bad counselors. If there was a famine in the land, the king had to work hard to feed his people. In his private life, he had to be a good husband and a good father. The responsibilities were almost too much for one man to bear.

According to the story in the Hebrew Scriptures, one night while King Solomon was dreaming, Yahweh appeared to him and said, "Ask for whatever you want me to give you" (1 Kings 3:5). Solomon replied, "Now, O LORD my God, you have made your servant king in place of my father David. But I am only a little child and do not know how to carry out my duties. Your servant is here among the people you have chosen, a great people, too numerous to count or number. So give your servant a discerning heart to govern your people and to distinguish between right and wrong. For who is able to govern this great people of yours?" (1 Kings 3:7-9).

Solomon asked nothing for himself, but only for what would benefit his people: wise leadership. According to the Scriptures, Yahweh told Solomon, "Since you have asked for this and not for long life or wealth for yourself, nor have asked for the death of your enemies but for discernment in administering justice, I will do what you have asked. I will give you a wise and discerning heart, so that there will never have been anyone like you, nor will there ever be. Moreover, I will give you what you have not asked for—both riches and honor—so that in your lifetime you will have no equal among kings" (1 Kings 3:11-13). As a result of Solomon's humble desire for and pursuit of knowledge, he was gifted with wisdom, and it is out of that wisdom that the many proverbs of Solomon were written.

With so much responsibility, Solomon did not have time to be lazy. From dawn to dark, he was busy taking care of his kingdom. Some of his most amusing proverbs

Lesson 4: First Chreia—King Solomon

were directed against lazy persons, known in the Hebrew Scriptures as sluggards. The word "sluggard" derives from the slow, fat, and slimy creatures known as slugs. Take a look at a few of those proverbs:

> How long will you lie there, you sluggard? When will you get up from your sleep? A little sleep, a little slumber, a little folding of the hands to rest— and poverty will come on you like a bandit and scarcity like an armed man. —Proverbs 6:9-11

> The way of the sluggard is blocked with thorns, but the path of the upright is a highway. —Proverbs 15:19

> The sluggard says, "There's a lion outside!" or, "I will be murdered in the streets!" —Proverbs 22:13

> The sluggard says, "There is a lion in the road, a fierce lion roaming the streets!" —Proverbs 26:13

> The sluggard buries his hand in the dish; he is too lazy to bring it back to his mouth. —Proverbs 26:15

For the purpose of this lesson's chreia, you will examine Proverbs 26:14: "As a door turns on its hinges, so a sluggard turns on his bed."

Tell It Back—Narration

Remember that a biography is a description of someone's life. Without looking at the biographical information about Solomon's life earlier in this lesson, tell back some of the most important details as best as you can remember them, keeping the details in the proper order. Keep in mind the five *W*s: who, what, when, where, and why.

The following are some questions to help you get started:

Who was King Solomon?

When and where did he live?

What did he do and what did he say?

Why did he do it and why did he say it?

Talk About It—

1. What is the literal (actual) meaning of the proverb "As a door turns on its hinges, so a sluggard turns on his bed"? How is figurative language (suggesting more than just the actual meaning) used?

2. How does King Solomon's life provide a good example of a hardworking person?

3. What is useful about Solomon's saying: "As a door turns on its hinges, so a sluggard turns on his bed"? Why is it important for a person to avoid laziness?

4. Can you think of any individual in history or in a story who was lazy, who didn't mind being lazy, and who did nothing to change his or her laziness? (This is the contrast portion of the chreia.)

5. Can you think of any individuals in history or in a story who worked hard to make good things happen? (This is the comparison portion of the chreia.)

Go Deeper—

For each question, circle or supply the correct answer(s).

1. Which of the following words (more than one) come close in meaning to the word "sluggard"?
   a. clown
   b. villain
   c. sloth
   d. lazybones
   e. loafer
   f. slouch

Lesson 4: First Chreia—King Solomon

2. Which of the following words (more than one) come close to meaning the opposite of a description of a sluggard?

   a. hard worker

   b. friend

   c. charmer

   d. diligent person

   e. laborer

3. What useful lesson can you learn from the previous short biography about King Solomon?

_____

_____

_____

_____

_____

4. Do you think it is generally true that hard-working people achieve more than lazy people? Why or why not?

_____

_____

_____

_____

_____

5. How is the following proverb similar to and different from "As a door turns on its hinges, so a sluggard turns on his bed"?

How long will you lie there, you sluggard? When will you get up from your sleep? A little sleep, a little slumber, a little folding of the hands to rest—and poverty will come on you like a bandit and scarcity like an armed man.
—Proverbs 6:9-11

_____

_____

_____

_____

_____

_____

_____

_____

_____

_____

_____

_____

Writing Time—

1. **DICTATION**—Your teacher will read a quote from the biographical information about King Solomon. Please listen carefully! After your teacher reads once, she will read slowly again and include the punctuation marks. Your task will be to write down the sentence as your teacher reads it.

_____

_____

_____

_____

2. **SENTENCE PLAY**—"When" is a question word used to ask about time. For example, the answer to "When can we play lacrosse?" might be "Three o'clock." The answer to "When did Charlemagne live?" is "He lived from 742 to 814." "When" can also be used to form statements about time. For example:

When she was a young woman, she dreamed of winning a gold medal at the Olympics. ("When" in this context means "at the time that she was a young woman.")

When you consider dying, old age doesn't seem so bad. ("When" in this context means "any time you consider dying.")

<u>When he was a young man, he felt overwhelmed by the responsibility of ruling a kingdom.</u> Follow this sentence pattern to create new "when" statements.

a. When Solomon fell asleep, _____

_____.

b. When the king went walking, _____

_____.

c. When we travel to the planet Mars, _____

_____.

d. When _____

_____.

3. **COPIOUSNESS**—In addition to working hard, King Solomon was a very rich ruler. Oh, yes! It is claimed that all of his drinking cups were made of pure gold. In order for you to write copiously, your sentences need to be rich as well. What makes a sentence rich? Detail!

Here's a very short sentence that lacks detail: "Solomon dreamed."

Now, this is a complete sentence. It has a subject and a predicate. A subject tells you whom or what the sentence is about. The **predicate** tells you what the subject does. Every complete sentence has these two main parts: subject and predicate. But just because the sentence is complete doesn't mean that it gives you enough detail. It isn't very rich. Don't you want to know who Solomon was? Don't you want to know what Solomon dreamed about? Try this: "King Solomon dreamed about building a glorious temple." Now that's more like it! This sentence is richer with detail.

A. Subjects and Predicates—Using the following subjects and predicates, build a sentence that includes at least one adjective and one adverb. Remember that an adjective describes the noun and the adverb describes the verb. Label the parts of speech as follows: *N* for noun, *ADJ* for adjective, *V* for verb, and *ADV* for adverb.

Example:

Subject: player

Predicate: kicks

ADJ   N   ADV V

Sentence: A football player rarely kicks a fifty-yard field goal.

i. Subject: sun

    Predicate: rises

_____

_____

ii. Subject: silver

    Predicate: arrived

_____

_____

iii. Subject: Solomon

    Predicate: dances

_____

_____

iv. Subject: cockroaches

    Predicate: run

_____

_____

v. Subject: tulips

    Predicate: will open

_____

_____

B. Adverbs—An adverb all by itself is very poor. It needs a sentence around it to reveal its usefulness and interest. Now let's create rich sentences out of a single adverb. Make sure your subjects are specific and your verbs are active. Remember that adverbs describe how, where, when, and how often something happens.

Example:
Adverb: diligently
Sentence: The envoy gathered the cedar diligently.

i. seldom

_____

_____

ii. forever

_____

_____

iii. somehow

_____

_____

iv. overseas

_____

_____

v. lightly

_____

_____

C. Prepositional Phrases—Another way to make a sentence rich is to add a prepositional phrase. Prepositions are often short words that show a time or space connection between words. A prepositional phrase begins with a preposition, such as "against all odds" and "down by the bank." They help us to answer the five *W*s: who, what, when, where, and why.

Add a prepositional phrase to the beginning or end of the following sentences using the preposition in the parentheses.

Example: The sun's light shimmers _____. (upon)
Change to: The sun's light shimmers upon the wall of stone.

Example: _____, the horse galloped hard. (at)
Change to: At his rider's command, the horse galloped hard.

i. The gold glittered brightly _____

_____. (upon)

ii. _____

_____, the underdog team won the game. (against)

iii. Would you like some ice cream _____

_____? (in)

iv. _____

_____, the girl waved good-bye to her sweetheart. (with)

v. A stormy breeze is blowing _____

_____. (through)

4. **CHREIA**—Write your own chreia about Solomon by following the steps listed.

Paragraph 1—Praise King Solomon. Show how he lived his life differently than a sluggard turning on his bed.

_____

_____

_____

_____

_____

_____

Paragraph 2—Give a new interpretation of the saying "As a door turns on its hinges, so a sluggard turns on his bed." Use your own words to form a new proverb.

_____

_____

_____

_____

_____

_____

Paragraph 3—Why is this proverb useful? Give details to support your answer.

_____

_____

Lesson 4: First Chreia—King Solomon

_____

_____

_____

_____

Paragraph 4—Introduce a contrast. Think of an example of someone in history or in a story who was extremely lazy. Give your example in the form of a very short narrative or story.

_____

_____

_____

_____

_____

_____

Paragraph 5—Introduce a comparison. Now think of an example of someone in history or in a story who worked hard to make good things happen. Give your example in the form of a very short narrative or story.

_____

_____

_____

_____

_____

_____

Paragraph 6—Conclude with a brief epilogue. Remember, an epilogue is nothing more than a tidy ending for your essay. It is like the ribbon on a present that wraps up everything neatly. You can use your own life or your parents' lives as an example or conclude with any other relevant thoughts.

_____

_____

_____

_____

_____

_____

_____

Speak It—

Read your chreia to a circle of classmates or to your entire class using proper delivery (*lexis*). Receive feedback about both your ideas and your delivery, your substance and your style. Students should ask the following questions:

1. Based on the reasoning (*logos*) of the speech, are you convinced that King Solomon is worthy of a chreia? Be specific—why or why not?

2. Did the reader speak at a proper pace and with good volume?

3. Did the reader use good inflection—highs and lows—in her delivery?

Lesson 5 · · · · · · · · · · · · · ·

Second Chreia— King Arthur

King Arthur! Isn't he the young knight who pulls a sword out of a magical stone and suddenly finds himself king of England? Isn't he the young king who battles a huge knight and has his sword smashed, only to be saved by his magician friend, Merlin?

Yes, those are Arthur stories. Much of what we know about King Arthur's life is legendary.

▶ Do you remember from *Writing & Rhetoric: Narrative II* what a legend is?

The earliest author to record Arthur's exploits is Nennius, a Welsh monk of the ninth century who wrote a famous book known as *The History of the Britons* almost three hundred years after Arthur lived. According to Nennius, Arthur was a warrior chieftain who helped to drive the barbarian invaders away from Roman Britannia for a time.

You see, the Romans had conquered Britannia, and many of the Celtic peoples of the island had started to act like Romans. They built Roman buildings, such as bathhouses and villas, and used Roman coins. But then came the collapse of the

Roman Empire in the late fourth century. Angle and Saxon barbarians invaded Britannia at the same time that Rome was mobbed by Vandals and Goths. Faced with barbarians at the gates of their Italian cities, the Roman army mostly abandoned Britannia in the fifth century. There was nobody but the local Britons, a Celtic tribe, left to defend the island.

Nennius tells us: "At that time, the Saxons grew strong by virtue of their large number and increased in power in Britain. [They] crossed from the northern part of Britain to the kingdom of Kent. . . . Then Arthur, along with the kings of Britain, fought against the Saxons in those days, but Arthur himself was the military commander."

Arthur fought eleven desperate battles against the invading Saxons, but it was the twelfth battle that secured his victory. Nennius wrote: "The twelfth battle was on Mount Badon in which there fell in one day 960 men from one charge by Arthur; and no one struck them down except Arthur himself, and in all the wars he emerged as victor."

▶ Does this brief narrative seem legendary in places to you? If so, where?

Now take a look at the story of the Round Table from the fifth century AD.

King Arthur

—adapted from *Our Island Story* by H.E. Marshall

If you be of prowess and worthiness, you shall be a knight of the Table Round.
—King Arthur

It is said that Arthur not only drove the Saxons out of Britain, but that he conquered other islands and tribes until at last he ruled over thirty kingdoms. Then for some years there was peace.

During these years, Arthur did much for his people. He taught them to love truth and goodness and to be Christian and gentle. No king had ever been loved as Arthur was loved.

In those fierce and far-off days, when men spent most of their time fighting, they were necessarily brave and strong in order to protect their dear ones, but they were very often cruel as well and nearly always fierce. Arthur taught people that it was possible to be brave yet kind, strong yet gentle. Many stories are told of the chivalry of Arthur and his daring knights, although they did not learn all their gentleness and their courtesy at once, as you shall hear.

Upon an Easter Day, Arthur called together all the knights and nobles from his many kingdoms for a great feast. They came from far and near—kings, earls, barons, and knights—gay in splendid clothes, glittering with jewels and gold.

As they waited for the king, they laughed and talked together, but secretly each heart was full of proud thoughts. Each man thought himself nobler and grander than any of the others.

The tables, covered with white silk cloths, were spread for the feast. Silver baskets piled with loaves, golden bowls, and cups full of wine stood ready, and as the knights and nobles talked and waited, they began to choose where they would sit.

In those days master and servants all sat together at the same table for meals. The master and his family sat at the top of the table, and the servants and poor people sat at the bottom of the table. So it came to be considered that the seats near the top were the best. The farther down the table anyone sat, the less honor was paid him.

At this feast only nobles were going to sit at table, yet everyone present wanted places at the top. "We will not sit in the seats of **scullions** and beggars," they said.

So they began to push each other aside and to say, "Make way; this is my seat."

"Nay, I am more honorable than you. You must sit below me."

"How dare you? My name is more noble than yours. That is my seat."

"Give place, I say."

At first it was only words, but soon it came to blows. They had come to the feast unarmed, so they had only their hands with which to fight, but as they grew angrier and angrier, they seized the bowls of wine and threw them at each other. Next the loaves of bread and the gold and silver cups were thrown about, the tables and benches were overturned, howls and yells filled the hall, and everything was in dreadful confusion.

When the noise was at its worst, the door opened and the king appeared. His face was stern and dignified as he looked down on the struggling, yelling crowd.

"Sit ye, sit ye down quickly, every man in the place where he is," he cried. "Whoso will not, he shall be put to death."

At the sound of their king's stern voice, the foolish nobles were filled with shame. Silently they sat down; the tables and benches were put back in their places, and the feast began.

But Arthur was sad at heart. "How can I teach my people to be gentle and kind if my knights will not even sit at meat in peace?" he said to himself. Then, as he sat sorrowfully wondering what he could do, Merlin the wizard came to him.

"Be not sad, O king," Merlin said, "but listen to my advice. Tell your carpenters to make a great round table at which there shall be a place for every knight. Then there can be no more quarrelling. For at a round table there is neither top nor bottom, so no knight can say that he sits above or below another. All shall be equal."

Then Arthur was sad no longer. He did as Merlin advised and had a great, round table made, at which there was a seat for each one of his knights. After that there was no more quarrelling as to who should have the best place, for all were equal, and Arthur's knights became known as the Knights of the Round Table.

But, alas! The time of peace did not last. Again came days of war and strife. In a great and terrible battle, Arthur and nearly all his knights were killed. Once more the fierce Saxons swept over the land, filling it with sorrow and bloodshed, and the nobility and beauty of knighthood were forgotten in Britain.

But some people think that Arthur did not die. They say that when he was wounded so that he could fight no more, the wise fairies came to take him back to fairyland. They say that he is still there, and that some day he will come again.

Other people say the stories about Arthur and his knights are not true, but at least we may believe that in those far-off, fierce, fighting days there was a king who taught his people that to be gentle was not cowardly and that to be cruel was not brave.

> Who reverenced his conscience as his king;
> Whose glory was **redressing** human wrong;
> Who spake no slander, no, nor listened to it,
> Who loved one only and who **clave** to her.
> —from *Idylls of the King* by Lord Alfred Tennyson

Tell It Back—Narration

Without looking at the biographical information about King Arthur found earlier in this lesson, tell back some of the most important details as best as you can remember them, keeping these details in the order they were told. Keep in mind the five *W*s: who, what, when, where, and why.

Here are some questions to help you get started:

- Who was King Arthur?
- When and where did he live?
- What did he do and what did he say?
- Why did he do it and why did he say it?

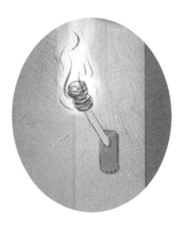

Talk About It—

1. What is a biography?

2. In one story about King Arthur, the king says, "If you be of prowess and worthiness, you shall be a knight of the Table Round." Thus King Arthur set two standards for the soldiers closest to him: prowess and worthiness. If a knight wanted to join Arthur's company, he had to have skill and strength (prowess) as well as bravery and honor (worthiness). Why is it wise that King Arthur didn't just choose knights who were good at fighting? Why didn't King Arthur just choose knights who were honorable?

3. How does King Arthur's life provide a good example of someone with prowess (skill) and worthiness (honor)?

4. What is useful about Arthur's saying: "If you be of prowess and worthiness, you shall be a knight of the Table Round"? Why is it important for someone to have prowess? What does it mean to be worthy or honorable?

5. Can you think of any individual in history or in a story who was a dishonorable or bloodthirsty soldier or who lacked fighting skill? (This is the contrast portion of the chreia.)

6. Can you think of any soldiers in history or in a story who were both skillful and honorable? (This is the comparison portion of the chreia.)

Go Deeper—

For each question, circle or supply the correct answer(s).

1. Why does a round table suggest that everyone at the table can be equal?
   a. because it is made of wood
   b. because there is no head of the table
   c. because everyone can all face each other
   d. because of its sturdy legs
   e. because everyone's position is the same

2. The English word "equal" comes from the Latin word *aequus*. Which of the following are synonyms for the word "equal"?
   a. best
   b. balanced
   c. same
   d. proud

3. Have you ever tried to insist on receiving greater honor and recognition than your classmates or friends? Have you ever seen someone else demand greater honor than others? Is it honorable to demand honor from others? Why or why not?

_____

_____

_____

_____

4. Who can you think of—either personally or from your reading—who has dignity and honor similar to Arthur's?

_____

_____

_____

_____

5. The biography does not explain what might have happened in Arthur's childhood to shape him into such a great leader and man of honor. Do you have an idea of what might have happened?

_____

_____

_____

_____

6. Of the following words, circle the one that best defines "prowess."

   a. excitement

   b. skill

   c. prowling

   d. progress

Writing Time—

1. **DICTATION**—Your teacher will read a quote from the previous information about King Arthur. Please listen carefully! After your teacher reads once, she will read slowly again and include the punctuation marks. Your task will be to write down the sentence as your teacher reads it.

   _____

   _____

   _____

   _____

2. **SENTENCE PLAY**—

   A. <u>They came from far and near—kings, earls, barons, and knights—glittering with jewels and gold.</u> Sentences can be made more interesting by adding lists to them. In this case, it's a list of nobles from the Middle Ages, but the author could have used magical creatures instead. For example: "They came from far and near—trolls, dragons, elves, and pixies—glittering with jewels and gold." You see, you can add all sorts of strange and wonderful details in a list! Using this sentence as a model, and using the suggestions in parentheses to create your lists, write other sentences in the same style. Examples: Arthur sat down to eat many things—mutton, chicken, bread, and wine—laughing as he chewed.

   Arthur's knights learned to fight with swords, spears, lances, and axes, preparing to defend the kingdom.

i. Arthur taught his subjects four virtues—_____,

_____, _____, and

_____—knowing that these virtues would
create a strong kingdom.
(four virtues)

ii. The servants set the tables for the feast with

_____, _____,

_____, and _____, mak-
ing everything look beautiful.
(four things on the tables)

iii. The girls liked to play _____,

_____, _____, and

_____, never pausing to consider ice hockey.
(four sports)

iv. Using the example as a guide, write your own sentence, being sure to
include a list.

_____

_____

_____

_____

_____

B. <u>As they waited for the king, they laughed and talked together, but secretly</u> <u>each heart was full of proud thoughts.</u> This sentence is very interesting because three things are happening at once. While the knights are waiting for the king, they are laughing and talking. But what else is going on in their hearts?

Using this sentence as a model, write other sentences in the same style. Remember that you want two or three things to be happening at once. If you like, use ideas from the Arthur story to invent your sentences. Example: As Arthur poured the wine, he saw the nobles arguing about the seating, but he wisely considered how to address it.

i. _____

_____

_____

ii. _____

_____

_____

iii. _____

_____

3. **COPIOUSNESS**—

A. <u>In those fierce and far-off days, when men spent most of their time fighting,</u>

<u>they were necessarily brave and strong.</u>

There's quite a wagonload of information in this sentence! It tells us that the days were violent (fierce) and that they happened a long time ago. And when days were fierce like that, men needed to be brave and strong and good fighters. How does a reasonably short sentence pack so much in? Adjectives! The sentence is loaded with four adjectives.

Label the four adjectives in the sentence with *ADJ* and then write a new sentence replacing them with other adjectives that are synonyms. Be sure to rewrite the entire sentence to gain practice in sentence construction.

_____

_____

_____

B. <u>In those fierce and far-off days, when men spent most of their time fighting, they were necessarily brave and strong.</u>

Besides adjectives, this sentence also uses adverbs and a verb to help us to see what those far-off days were like. Label the two adverbs, as well as the verb "fighting," and replace these words with synonyms.

_____

_____

_____

C. <u>But, alas! The time of peace did not last.</u> Rewrite this selection using different words, but express the same idea. How might you say "alas," "time," "peace," and "did not last" differently? For example, instead of "alas" you might use phrases such as "what a shame" or "too bad."

_____

_____

_____

D. Erasmus said, "Write, write, and again write." In other words, rarely settle for the first draft of anything. Always push yourself to use more specific words.

Examine the painting of *Saint George and the Dragon*. This picture illustrates the strength of one man standing courageously against a fearsome foe. The following descriptions of this painting are weak. Write more interesting descriptions using the prompts provided.

Saint George's armor is cool.

Think of comparisons that would give a better picture of the armor. These comparisons, using the words "like" or "as," are known as similes.

Examples: Saint George's armor shines like a candle in the dark.
Saint George's armor is as strong as the shell of an armadillo.

i. Saint George's armor shines like _____

_____.

ii. Saint George's armor is as strong as _____

_____.

The dragon looks nasty.

This description tells us almost nothing about the dragon. Does the dragon look hungry, angry, fierce, or sinister? Is he large or small, thick or snake-like? What about his teeth or claws? Give a detailed description of the dragon using color, texture, and other observations.

_____

_____

_____

_____

_____

4. **CHREIA**—Write your own chreia about King Arthur by following the steps listed.
   Paragraph 1—Praise King Arthur. Show how he lived up to his standard of a knight with prowess and worthiness. Use the story to provide details but use your own insight and way of speaking.

Paragraph 2—Give a new version of the statement "If you be of prowess and worthiness, you shall be a knight of the Table Round." Use figurative language if you like.

_____

_____

_____

_____

_____

_____

_____

_____

_____

Paragraph 3—Why is this statement useful? Give details to support your answer.

_____

_____

_____

_____

_____

_____

_____

_____

Lesson 5: *Second Chreia—King Arthur*

Paragraph 4—Introduce a contrast. Think of an example of someone in history or in a story who was a dishonorable or bloodthirsty soldier or who lacked fighting skill. Give your example in the form of a very short narrative or story.

_____

_____

_____

_____

_____

_____

_____

_____

_____

Paragraph 5—Introduce a comparison. Now think of an example of someone in history or in a story who showed both prowess in battle and worthiness in character. Give your example in the form of a very short narrative or story.

_____

_____

_____

_____

_____

_____

_____

_____

_____

Lesson 5: Second Chreia—King Arthur

Paragraph 6—Conclude with a brief epilogue. Remember, an epilogue is nothing more than a tidy ending for your essay. It is like the ribbon on a present that wraps up everything neatly. You can use your own life or your parents' lives as an example or conclude with any other relevant thoughts.

_____

_____

_____

_____

_____

_____

_____

_____

_____

Speak It—

Read your chreia to a circle of classmates or to your entire class or into a recording device using proper delivery (*lexis*). Receive feedback about both your ideas and your delivery, your substance and your style. Note the places in your essay where you might make a few changes to make it smoother or more precise. Listening students should ask the following questions:

1. Based on the reasoning (*logos*) of the speech, are you convinced that King Arthur is worthy of a chreia? Be specific—why or why not?

2. Did the reader speak at a proper pace and with good volume? Did the reader use good inflection—high and lows—in her delivery?

Lesson 5: Second Chreia—King Arthur

Lesson 6 ·········

Third Chreia— King Alfred the Great

The saddest thing about any man is that he be ignorant, and the most exciting thing is that he knows. —Alfred, king of England from 871–899

Can you find the town of Wantage on a map of England? It is in the south-central region of the island in a county now called Oxfordshire, exactly west of London. The university town of Oxford is nearby, just to the northeast of Wantage. It was in Wantage that King Alfred, the greatest of all English kings, was born.

The English loved King Alfred. He was one of those rare men who achieved great things in everything he did. He was a great fighter and a great leader of armies, and today he is most famous for stopping the Viking invasion of his island. Back in the ninth century AD, it looked as if the Vikings would easily gobble up England. However, Alfred was able to unite the weak English kingdoms and drive the powerful Vikings to a pocket in the eastern part of the island.

But Alfred was much more than a great leader in battle. He was also a great judge and lawgiver, a great translator of books, a great scholar, and a man devoted to his faith in God.

The following story illustrates Alfred's love for learning.

Young Alfred and the Book

—based on *Fifty Famous People* by James Baldwin

A thousand years ago, most boys and girls did not learn to read. Books were very scarce and very precious, and only a few men and women could read them. Each book was written with a pen or a brush. The pictures were painted by hand, and some of them were very beautiful. A good book would sometimes cost as much as a good house.

In those times there were even some kings who could not read. They thought more of hunting and fighting than of learning.

There was one such king who had four sons: Ethelbald, Ethelbert, Ethelred, and Alfred. The three older boys were sturdy, half-grown lads; the youngest, Alfred, was a slender, fair-haired child.

One day when the boys were with their mother, she showed them a wonderful book that a rich friend had given her. She turned the leaves and showed them the strange letters. She showed them the beautiful pictures and told them how they had been drawn and painted.

The boys admired the book very much, for they had never seen anything like it.

"But the best part of it is the story that it tells," said their mother. "If you could only read, you might learn that story and enjoy it. Now I have a mind to give this book to one of you."

"Will you give it to me, Mother?" asked little Alfred.

"I will give it to the one who first learns to read in it," she answered.

"I am sure I would rather have a good bow with arrows," said Ethelred.

"And I would rather have a young hawk that has been trained to hunt," said Ethelbert.

"If I were a priest or a monk," said Ethelbald, "I would learn to read. But I am a prince, and it is foolish for princes to waste their time with such things."

"But I should like to know the story that this book tells," said Alfred.

A few months passed by. Then, one morning, Alfred went into his mother's room with a smiling, joyous face.

"Mother," he said, "will you let me see that beautiful book again?"

His mother unlocked her cabinet and took the precious volume from its place of safekeeping.

Alfred opened it with careful fingers. Then he began with the first word on the first page and read the first story aloud without making one mistake.

"O my child, how did you learn to do that?" cried his mother.

"I asked the monk, Brother Felix, to teach me," said Alfred. "And every day since you showed me the book, he has given me a lesson. It was no easy thing to learn these letters and how they are put together to make words. Now Brother Felix says I am learning to read almost as well as he."

"How wonderful!" said his mother.

"How foolish!" said Ethelbald.

"You will be a good monk when you grow up," said Ethelred with a sneer.

But his mother kissed Alfred and gave him the beautiful book. "The prize is yours, Alfred," she said. "I am sure that whether you grow up to be a monk or a king, you will be a wise and noble man."

And Alfred did grow up to become the wisest and noblest king that England ever had. In history he is called Alfred the Great.

The inscription on Alfred's statue in Wantage says:

> Alfred found learning dead,
> and he restored it.
> Education neglected,
> and he revived it.
> The laws powerless,
> and he gave them force.
> The Church debased,
> and he raised it.
> The land ravaged by a fearful enemy,
> from which he delivered it.
> Alfred's name will live as long
> as mankind shall respect the past.

Tell It Back—Narration

1. Oral narration: Without looking at the text, tell the story of *Young Alfred and the Book* as best as you remember it using your own words. Try not to leave out any important detail. Here is the first sentence to help you get started: "A thousand years ago most boys and girls did not learn to read."

2. Outline: Create a simple outline for the story of *Young Alfred and the Book* using Roman numerals (*I, II, III*) for the most important events and capital letters (*A, B, C*) for less important events. Use standard numbers (*1, 2, 3*) for minor points.

Talk About It—

1. What are some things you admire about King Alfred?

2. What does it mean to be ignorant?

3. Examine the picture of the statue of Alfred in the town of Wantage. What do you think the sculptor is saying about what is most important to Alfred? Notice the difference between the positions of the battle ax in one hand and the scroll of learning in the other.

4. How does Alfred's life provide a good example of someone who was eager for knowledge? Why did Alfred's brothers remain ignorant?

5. What is useful about Alfred's saying: "The saddest thing about any man is that he be ignorant, and the most exciting thing is that he knows"? Why is it important for a person to know that he or she is ignorant?

6. Can you think of anybody in history or in a story who was ignorant, who didn't mind being ignorant, and who did nothing to change his ignorance? (This is the contrast portion of the chreia.)

7. Can you think of anybody in history or in a story who desired knowledge and learning and who worked hard to gain knowledge? (This is the comparison portion of the chreia.)

Go Deeper—

For each question, circle or supply the correct answer(s).

1. Our word "ignorant" comes from the Latin word *ignarus*, which means "unaware" or "unknown." From *ignarus* we also get our words "ignore" and "ignorance." Which of the following words come close to the meaning of "ignorant"?

   a. unschooled
   b. unlikely
   c. unaware
   d. untaught
   e. untrained
   f. unlovely
   g. uneducated

2. Another word that can mean "ignorant" is "illiterate." The Latin word *littera* means "letter," so to be illiterate means to be "without letters." If you are illiterate, without the knowledge of letters, can you read books? Who taught Alfred his letters?

   _____

   _____

   _____

   _____

3. Someone who can read letters (and the words they make) can be called literate. If you can read this sentence, then you are literate! Which of the following words come close to the meaning of "literate" (able to read)?
   a. uneducated
   b. educated
   c. bored
   d. schooled
   e. instructed
   f. lettered
   g. thoughtful
   h. humorous

4. What caused Alfred to become interested in learning to read? What caused you to become interested in learning to read?

   _____

   _____

   _____

   _____

Writing Time—

1. **DICTATION**—Your teacher will read a quote from the previous information about King Alfred. Please listen carefully! After your teacher reads once, she will read slowly again and include the punctuation marks. Your task will be to write down the sentence as your teacher reads it.

   _____

   _____

   _____

   _____

2. **SENTENCE PLAY**—

A. <u>A good book would sometimes cost as much as a good house.</u> In this sentence, the word "as" helps to make a comparison between a book and a house. With this sentence as a model, use the supplied phrases to create sentences that make new comparisons.

Example: as well as
A young boy can read as well as a monk.

i.   as low as

_____

_____

ii. as smart as

_____

_____

iii. as nasty as

_____

_____

iv. as lovely as

_____

_____

v. Write your own sentence using an "as" phrase.

_____

_____

B. <u>In those times there were even some kings who could not read. They thought more of hunting and fighting than of learning.</u> Notice how the second sentence explains the first. It's hard to believe that some kings could not read during the Middle Ages. Of course, they had plenty of other things on their minds. The reason some kings did not learn to read was because they liked hunting and fighting better.

Using these two sentences as a model, write other sentences in the same style, with the second sentence explaining the first.

Examples:
In those days, there were even some queens who could not dance. They thought more of archery and riding horses than of dancing.
During the winter, Alfred did not learn to dance. He thought more of reading and books than of dancing.

i. _____

_____

ii. _____

_____

iii. _____

_____

C. Label the prepositions (*PREP*) and adjectives (*ADJ*) in the following sentence.

Alfred went into his mother's room with a smiling, joyous face.

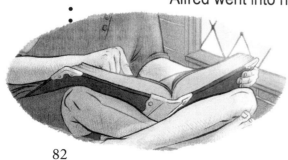

Lesson 6: Third Chreia—King Alfred the Great

Using this sentence as a model, write some new sentences in the same style, describing the action with one or two phrases beginning with prepositions (such as "until," "with," "through," "toward," "over," "in," "as," "by," "of," etc).

                              PREP   PREP   ADJ   ADJ
Example: Mei Li walked through the forest with a frisky, happy panda.

i. _____

_____

ii. _____

_____

iii. _____

_____

3. **COPIOUSNESS**—

A. Take a look at the following sentences about Alfred and make them stronger and sharper. Mark the adjectives with *ADJ* and the nouns with *N*. Change and intensify (strengthen and sharpen) the adjectives and change the common nouns to make them more specific.

                      ADJ   N   ADJ   N
Example: Alfred was a good man as well as a good fighter.
Change to: Alfred was a wise king as well as a fearless war chief.

i. Alfred was forced to hide from mean people and disguise himself as a poor guy.

_____

_____

ii. While hiding in a dwelling, Alfred accidentally burned some nice cake over a warm flame.

_____

_____

iii. An old woman scolded him for being such a lazy, bad person.

_____

_____

iv. When the poor female discovered that Alfred was really her good leader, she bowed and said, "My brave guy, my leader."

_____

_____

B. King Alfred used strong Old English verbs such as "ache," "bake," "cram," "dare," and "hang." The sentences in this section contain weak verbs. Mark the verbs with *V* and make them more specific with the suggested verb. Add the adverb in parentheses at an appropriate place in the sentence. The sentence may be rewritten as needed to work with the stronger verb.

Example: Quill pens were taken from dead swans and geese. plucked / (usually)
Change to: Quill pens were usually plucked from dead swans and geese.

i. In the Middle Ages, monks made books with quill pens. wrote /(slowly)

_____

_____

ii. Few people could see books let alone have them. read / own (ever)

_____

_____

iii. Stained glass and painted altarpieces were Bible stories for illiterate people. told / (often)

_____

_____

iv. This church art is said to be the Poor Man's Bible. is called / (today)

_____

_____

C. The following sentence gets the job done, but it could be more interesting.

She showed them the <u>beautiful</u> <u>picture</u> and <u>said</u> how it had been <u>made</u>.

How can it be improved? By making the nouns, verbs, and adjectives more specific and more intense, that's how! First, label the underlined noun, verbs, and adjective. Next, replace them (you don't have to use synonyms) and rewrite the sentence.

Ask yourself:
• What adjectives are more descriptive than "beautiful"? (Think of both positive and negative words.)
• What nouns are more specific than "picture"?
• What are specific ways to say something or to make something?

Example: She showed them the colorful photograph and explained how it had been shot.

i. _____

_____

ii. _____

_____

4. **CHREIA**—Write your own chreia about King Alfred by following the steps listed.

Paragraph 1—Praise King Alfred. Show how he lived his life according to the principles in his saying.

_____

_____

_____

_____

_____

_____

Paragraph 2—Give a new version of the saying, "The saddest thing about any man is that he be ignorant, and the most exciting thing is that he knows." Use your own words to rephrase Alfred's saying to show that you understand it.

_____

_____

_____

_____

_____

Lesson 6: *Third Chreia—King Alfred the Great*

Paragraph 3—Why is this saying useful? Give details to support your answer.

_____

_____

_____

_____

_____

_____

_____

Paragraph 4—Introduce a contrast. Think of an example of someone in history or in a story who didn't mind being ignorant. Give your example in the form of a very short narrative or story.

_____

_____

_____

_____

_____

_____

Paragraph 5—Introduce a comparison. Now think of an example of someone in history or in a story who desired knowledge to overcome ignorance. Give your example in the form of a very short narrative or story.

_____

_____

_____

Lesson 6: Third Chreia—King Alfred the Great

_____

_____

_____

_____

_____

_____

_____

Paragraph 6—Conclude with a brief epilogue. Remember, an epilogue is nothing more than a tidy ending for your essay. It is like the ribbon on a present that wraps up everything neatly. You can use your own life as an example or conclude with any other relevant thoughts.

_____

_____

_____

_____

_____

_____

5. **NARRATIVE PRACTICE**—In *Writing & Rhetoric: Narrative II*, you learned that conflict makes the middle of a story more interesting. The following passage contains dialogue between young Alfred and his brothers that introduces the conflict of the story: Alfred's brothers do not have much interest in the beautiful book and later tease Alfred for learning to read.

The boys admired the book very much, for they had never seen anything like it.

Lesson 6: Third Chreia—King Alfred the Great

"But the best part of it is the story that it tells," said their mother. "If you could only read, you might learn that story and enjoy it. Now I have a mind to give this book to one of you."

"Will you give it to me, Mother?" asked little Alfred.

"I will give it to the one who first learns to read in it," she answered.

"I am sure I would rather have a good bow with arrows," said Ethelred.

"And I would rather have a young hawk that has been trained to hunt," said Ethelbert.

"If I were a priest or a monk," said Ethelbald, "I would learn to read. But I am a prince, and it is foolish for princes to waste their time with such things."

"But I should like to know the story that this book tells," said Alfred.

Alfred is the protagonist, or leading character, of this story, while his brothers are antagonists, the characters that oppose the protagonist. Using the previous passage as a model, write a short stretch of dialogue between a character and his brothers or sisters, including conflict in the dialogue. Use one of the following beginnings or make up your own:

The girls admired the bicycle very much, for they had never seen anything like it.

The boys admired the guitar very much, for they had never seen anything like it.

The dogs admired the pork chop very much, for they had never tasted anything like it.

_____

_____

_____

_____

_____

_____

_____

Speak It—

The following is a famous speech by another great king of England, Henry V, as written by William Shakespeare. In the speech, Henry V passionately challenges his disheartened troops on the day of the Battle of Agincourt, trying to stir their fighting spirit against a stronger French army in the same way Alfred tried to stir his people to become learned. The *logos*, or content, is already there for you. Try delivering the speech aloud with plenty of *lexis*, or style. Practice it a few times before your presentation. After you finish, watch the stupendous delivery of the St. Crispin's Day speech by Kenneth Branagh in the film *Henry V*. How did you compare?

> If we are mark'd to die, we are **enow**
>
> To do our country loss; and if to live,
>
> The fewer men, the greater share of honor.
>
> God's will! I pray thee, wish not one man more.
>
> By Jove, I am not covetous for gold,
>
> Nor care I who doth feed upon my cost;
>
> It yearns me not if men my garments wear;
>
> Such outward things dwell not in my desires:
>
> But if it be a sin to covet honor,
>
> I am the most offending soul alive.
>
> No, faith, my coz, wish not a man from England:
>
> God's peace! I would not lose so great an honor
>
> As one man more, methinks, would share from me
>
> For the best hope I have. O, do not wish one more!
>
> Rather proclaim it, Westmoreland, through my host,
>
> That he which hath no stomach to this fight,
>
> Let him depart; his passport shall be made
>
> And crowns for convoy put into his purse:
>
> We would not die in that man's company
>
> That fears his fellowship to die with us.

This day is called the feast of Crispian:

He that outlives this day, and comes safe home,

Will stand a tip-toe when the day is named,

And rouse him at the name of Crispian.

He that shall live this day, and see old age,

Will yearly on the vigil feast his neighbors,

And say 'To-morrow is Saint Crispian:'

Then will he strip his sleeve and show his scars.

And say 'These wounds I had on Crispin's day.'

Old men forget: yet all shall be forgot,

But he'll remember with advantages

What feats he did that day: then shall our names.

Familiar in his mouth as household words

Harry the king, Bedford and Exeter,

Warwick and Talbot, Salisbury and Gloucester,

Be in their flowing cups freshly remember'd.

This story shall the good man teach his son;

And Crispin Crispian shall ne'er go by,

From this day to the ending of the world,

But we in it shall be remember'd;

We few, we happy few, we band of brothers;

For he to-day that sheds his blood with me

Shall be my brother; be he ne'er so vile,

This day shall gentle his condition:

And gentlemen in England now a-bed

Shall think themselves accursed they were not here,

And hold their manhoods cheap whiles any speaks

That fought with us upon Saint Crispin's day.

Lesson 7 ·············

Fourth Chreia— King Canute

Learn how feeble is the power of earthly kings. None is worthy of the name of king but He whom heaven and earth and sea obey. —King Canute

In the last lesson you learned about King Alfred the Great of England and studied England on a map. "England," by the way, means "Angle-land" or "the land of the Angles and Saxons." Now that you know where England is on the map, try to find Denmark.

Beginning in 787, Vikings came from Denmark to attack the rich lands to the south. They came in their long ships, wave after wave, and plundered monasteries and coastal towns. They were able, at last, to defeat the Anglo-Saxons and establish their own kingdoms in England.

Two hundred years later, Canute (kuh-noot), a Danish Viking, was king of England from 1014–1035. Over time Canute conquered the lands of Norway and Sweden and added them to his English and Danish kingdom. He rebuilt churches that had been destroyed by the Vikings of the past and gave generous gifts to monasteries. He traveled to Rome to visit the pope, the head of the church, to show that he was obedient to the pope's teachings. Like King Alfred, Canute encouraged peace and learning among his people.

While Canute was a rough-and-tumble warrior, he was also serious about showing that "earthly kings" were not all-powerful. Take a look at one story from the time of Canute's reign that demonstrates this principle.

King Canute and the Sea

—adapted from *Fifty Famous Stories Retold* by James Baldwin

A hundred years or more after the time of Alfred the Great, there was a king of England named Canute. King Canute was a Dane. The Danes were not so fierce and cruel then as they had been when they were at war with King Alfred.

The great men and ladies who were around King Canute were always praising him. "You are the greatest man who ever lived," one would say.

Then another would say, "O king, there can never be another man so mighty as you."

And another would say, "Great Canute, there is nothing in the world that dares to disobey you."

The king was a man of sense, and he grew very tired of hearing such foolish speeches. One day he was by the seashore, and his officers were with him. They were praising him, as they were in the habit of doing. He thought that now he would teach them a lesson, and so he bade them set his chair on the beach close by the edge of the water.

"Am I the greatest man in the world?" he asked.

"O king!" they cried, "There is no one so mighty as you."

"Do all things obey me?" he asked.

"There is nothing that dares to disobey you, O king!" they said. "The world bows before you and gives you honor."

"Will the sea obey me?" he asked, and he looked down at the little waves that were lapping the sand at his feet.

The foolish officers were puzzled, but they did not dare to say, "No." "Command it, O king, and it will obey," said one.

"Sea," cried Canute, "I command you to come no farther! Waves, stop your rolling, and do not dare to touch my feet!"

But the tide came in, just as it always did. The water rose higher and higher. It came up around the king's chair and wet not only his feet but also his robe. His officers stood about him, alarmed and wondering whether he was not mad.

With a stern face, Canute turned to his officers and said, "Learn how feeble is the power of earthly kings. None is worthy of the name of king but He whom heaven and earth and sea obey."

Tell It Back—Narration

1. Oral narration: Without looking at the text, tell the story of *King Canute and the Sea* as best as you remember it using your own words. Try not to leave out any important detail. Here is the first sentence to help you get started: "A hundred years or more after the time of Alfred the Great there was a king of England named Canute."

2. Outline: Create a simple outline for the story of *King Canute and the Sea* using Roman numerals (*I, II, III*) for the most important events and capital letters (*A, B, C*) for less important events. Use standard numbers (*1, 2, 3*) for minor points.

Talk About It—

1. What is Canute's problem with his nobles and officers? Why would a king want his advisors to be different from Canute's?

2. How does Canute show them their foolishness?

3. What is useful about Canute's saying: "Learn how feeble is the power of earthly kings. None is worthy of the name of king but He whom heaven and earth and sea obey"?

4. Can you think of anybody in history or in a story who thought too highly of human power? (This is the contrast portion of the chreia.)

5. Can you think of anybody in history or in a story who was a humble ruler or leader? (This is the comparison portion of the chreia.)

6. Examine the painting *King Canute Defies the Waves* by James Edwin McConnell. How would you describe the faces of the people watching the waves? Why are those people foolish?

▲ *King Canute Defies the Waves*, an etching taken from a Victorian newpaper, 1868.

Go Deeper—

For each question, circle or supply the correct answer(s).

1. Which one of the following three words do you think comes closest to describing the kind of false praise that those around King Canute gave him? You may look up the words in the dictionary if you do not know their differences in meaning.

   a. compliment

   b. appreciation

   c. flattery

2. Why do you think some people are tempted to shower powerful kings and leaders with exaggerated praise? Why did Canute dislike this kind of praise?

_____

_____

_____

_____

3. Have you ever praised someone beyond what was true? What tempted you to do so?

_____

_____

_____

_____

4. If this story of King Canute and the waves was a fable, what do you think the moral would be? In other words, what should you learn from this story?

_____

_____

_____

_____

Writing Time—

1. **DICTATION**—Your teacher will read a quote from the narrative about King Canute. Please listen carefully! After your teacher reads once, she will read slowly again and include the punctuation marks. Your task will be to write down the sentence as your teacher reads it.

_____

_____

_____

_____

_____

2. **SENTENCE PLAY**—"<u>Waves, stop your rolling!</u>" This command may be a little unusual, but it is very strong. This is because it names the object being commanded. The sentence would not be as strong if Canute had simply said, "Stop your rolling!" Using this sentence as a model, create other commands that name the object.

Example: Write a command about cars.
   "Cars, stop your honking!"

a. Write a command about a horse.

_____

_____

b. Write a command about feet.

_____

_____

c. Write a command about a barber.

_____

_____

d. Write a command about storm clouds.

_____

_____

e. Write a command about Natalie, who shouts.

_____

_____

3. **COPIOUSNESS—**

"You are the greatest man who ever lived," one would say.

Then another would say, "O king, there can never be another man so mighty as you."

And another would say, "Great Canute, there is nothing in the world that dares to disobey you."

Notice how the three previous quotations all seek to flatter the king, telling him that no one is as powerful as he is. They really say the same thing using different words. That is what copiousness is all about—saying the same thing using a variety of words and sentences.

A. Write three quotations from three different people to wish someone a happy birthday. Use different words so that each sentence seems a little grander and more exaggerated than the last.

Example: One would say, "Happy birthday, friend."

Another would say, "Happy fantastic birthday, dear friend!"

And another would say, "Have an amazing birthday, best friend ever!"

i. One would say, "_____

_____."

ii. Then another would say, "_____

_____."

iii. And another would say, "_____

_____."

B. Write three quotations from three different people to encourage a sick person to feel better. Again, use different words so that each sentence seems a little grander and more exaggerated than the last.

i. One would say, "_____

_____."

ii. Then another would say, "_____

_____,

iii. And another would say, "_____

_____."

4. **CHREIA**—Write your own chreia about King Canute by following the steps listed.

Paragraph 1—Praise King Canute. Show how he lived his life according to the principles in his saying.

_____

_____

_____

_____

_____

_____

_____

_____

_____

Paragraph 2—Give a new version of the saying "Learn how feeble is the power of earthly kings. None is worthy of the name of king but He whom heaven and earth and sea obey." Use your own words to rephrase the saying to show that you understand it.

_____

_____

_____

_____

Paragraph 3—Why is this proverb useful? Give details to support your answer.

_____

_____

_____

_____

_____

_____

_____

_____

Paragraph 4—Introduce a contrast. Think of an example of someone in history or in a story who was greedy for power. Give your example in the form of a very short narrative or story.

_____

_____

_____

_____

_____

_____

_____

_____

_____

_____

_____

Paragraph 5—Introduce a comparison. Now think of an example of someone in history or in a story who lived by the wisdom of Canute's saying, who knew that he was not master of the universe. Give your example in the form of a very short narrative or story.

_____

_____

_____

_____

_____

_____

_____

_____

_____

_____

Paragraph 6—Conclude with a brief epilogue. Remember, an epilogue is nothing more than a tidy ending for your essay. It is like the ribbon on a present that wraps up everything neatly. You can use your own life as an example or conclude with any other relevant thoughts.

_____

_____

_____

_____

_____

_____

_____

_____

_____

Lesson 7: *Fourth Chreia—King Canute*

Speak It—

The following is a short play for you to perform. It dramatizes the story of *King Canute and the Sea* and uses some of the same dialogue from the narrative at the beginning of this lesson. Drama performances always require proper elocution, so remember to speak with good volume, to use inflection, and to pronounce each word clearly.

Cast

Chief 1

Chief 2

Great Lady

King Canute

Canute is being followed by two chiefs and a great lady of the court. The two chiefs carry a chair, and the great lady carries a bowl of fruit.

KING CANUTE: I love to walk along the beach.

CHIEF 1: Yes, sire. As do I!

CHIEF 2: A walk is just the thing!

GREAT LADY: How thrilling it must be for you, sire, to look across the ocean and see your entire great kingdom at once. Norway!

CHIEF 1: Denmark!

CHIEF 2: Sweden!

GREAT LADY: And England!

KING CANUTE: (stares across the water) Friends, I can only see water. Perhaps I'm not as great as you think I am.

The two chiefs place the chair on the ground. Canute sits.

CHIEF 1: Oh, no! You are the greatest man who ever lived.

CHIEF 2: O king, there can never be another man so mighty as you.

GREAT LADY: Great Canute, there is nothing in the world that dares to disobey you.

KING CANUTE: Hmmm. Is that so?

CHIEF 1, CHIEF 2, AND GREAT LADY: *(in unison)* Absolutely!

KING CANUTE: Well, now, so I'm the greatest man in the world?

CHIEF 1: O king, there is no one so mighty as you.

KING CANUTE: Do all things obey me?

CHIEF 2: There is nothing that dares to disobey you, O king! The world bows before you and gives you honor.

They all bow very low. The fruit falls from the bowl to the ground and the courtiers hastily pick it up.

KING CANUTE: Will the sea obey me?

GREAT LADY: Command it, O king, and it will obey.

KING CANUTE: Sea, I command you to come no farther! Waves, stop your rolling, and do not dare to touch my feet!

CHIEF 1: *(aside to others)* What is he doing?

CHIEF 2: *(aside to others)* Do you think he's lost his mind?

KING CANUTE: Ah! Ah! I'm getting my feet wet!

The three pick up the chair with the king in it and move it back.

KING CANUTE: Another wave!

The three pick up the chair again and move it back.

KING CANUTE: Now what do you say, you scoundrels? Learn how feeble is the power of earthly kings. None is worthy of the name of king but He whom heaven and earth and sea obey.

Canute rises from the chair and walks offstage.

Lesson 7: Fourth Chreia—King Canute

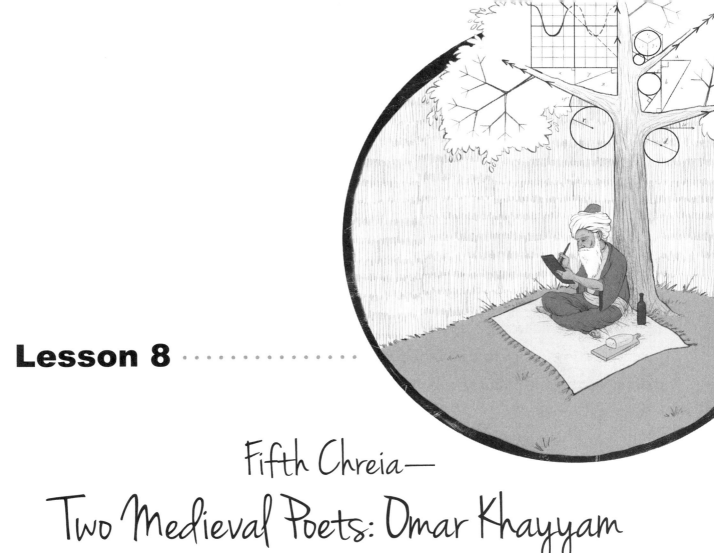

Lesson 8

Fifth Chreia—
Two Medieval Poets: Omar Khayyam and Thomas Tusser

Omar Khayyam, 1048–1131

Because "Khayyam" means "tentmaker," it is believed that Omar Khayyam was probably born into a family of prosperous tentmakers. His home country was Persia, which is known today as Iran. He was sent to study with some of the finest teachers in the region and worked diligently, especially in the subject he loved best: mathematics.

Khayyam worked hard all his life to improve our understanding of mathematics and the universe. His most famous work was in algebra and geometry, two fascinating branches of math. Algebra is a bit like puzzle-solving, using symbols to take the place of numbers. Geometry is the study of the size and position of shapes—everything from flat shapes like triangles to solid shapes like pyramids. Khayyam discovered new ways to solve complex problems involving cubes and circles.

He also enjoyed studying stars and helped improve the Persian calendar. He measured the length of the year so accurately (365.24219858156 days) that his calendar has only a one-day error every five thousand years. His love for astronomy, the study of the stars, shows up in many of his poems. It's his poetry that makes Omar Khayyam most famous today.

Khayyam wrote his poems in four lines that have typically been translated from Arabic into English with three rhyming lines and one line that doesn't rhyme. **Rhymes** are words that repeat the same sound pattern in some way and are usually placed at the ends of lines so that your ear begins to listen for them when you read or listen to a poem. The collection of four-lined poems that Khayyam wrote is known as the *Rubaiyat*.

The following are two examples of the *AABA* rhyming pattern. Notice how the *A* lines rhyme with each other, while the *B* lines (ending in the words "strikes" and "us") don't rhyme with the other lines' end words. (Note that there are many different kinds of rhyme: Some rhymes, called **full rhymes**, share many of the same letters or have exactly the same sounds. Other rhymes, called **slant rhymes**, are more distant, without the exact letters or sounds repeated, but you should still be able to detect a similarity between them.)

Wake! For the Sun, who scatter'd into flight	A
The Stars before him from the Field of Night,	A
Drives Night along with them from Heav'n, and strikes	B
The Sultan's Turret with a Shaft of Light.	A
Yon rising Moon that looks for us again—	A
How oft hereafter will she wax and wane;	A
How oft hereafter rising look for us	B
Through this same Garden—and for one in vain!	A

Even though mathematics and astronomy were hard work for Khayyam, these pursuits gave him great delight. He loved numbers and stargazing. He also delighted in the simple things in life, such as food, love, and poetry. His poetry seems to show that he was the kind of person who wouldn't need video games, blockbuster movies, and thrill rides to entertain him, even if they had been invented in the twelfth century.

Take a closer look at another poem in the *Rubaiyat*:

> Here with a Loaf of Bread beneath the **Bough**,   branch
> A Flask of Wine, a Book of Verse—and Thou
> Beside me singing in the Wilderness—
> And Wilderness is Paradise **enow**.   enough

▶ What do you think this poem means?

▶ Despite the desolation around him, the poet seems to be content. What does the poet have that makes him feel contented?

Thomas Tusser, 1524–1580

When he was just a boy, Thomas Tusser sang in one of the most important choirs in England, St. Paul's Cathedral choir. Later he sang and studied at Eton College and Cambridge University. Yet despite a promising career as a musician, Tusser longed to settle in the country and have a family, and so after his wedding Tusser put down roots as a farmer.

Most farmers in the sixteenth century were illiterate, meaning they could neither read nor write. Tusser not only could read and write, but he enjoyed jotting down the many proverbs he heard from the simple English country folk he knew. Eventually he turned these proverbs into rhymes and published *Five Hundred Points of Good Husbandry*, a book of poetry about the farmer's year. Tusser's rhymes capture his simple love for tilling the soil, planting plants, and sowing seeds, as you can see in the following poem:

> Set strawberries, wife,
> I love them for life.

Plant **respe** and rose,   raspberries

And such as those. . . .

First barley, then peas,

Then wheat, if ye please.

Tusser clearly loved watching the weather as well:

North winds send hail, south winds bring rain,

East winds we bewail, west winds blow **amain**;   at full speed

North-east is too cold, south-east not too warm,

North-west is too bold, south-west doth no harm.

Tusser gave us many fine proverbs, including "A fool and his money are soon parted" and "Sweet April showers do spring May flowers." Most of his poems are just good advice about farming such as, "Let hog, once fat, Lose nothing of that" or "Let sheep fill flank, Where corn is too rank." But other times Tusser was more thoughtful and wrote about what it's like to be human:

The year I compare, as I find for a truth,

The Spring unto Childhood, the Summer to Youth.

The Harvest to Manhood, the Winter to Age,

All quickly forgot, as a play on a stage.

Other times he urged people to have fun, such as in this good advice:

At Christmas play and make good cheer,

For Christmas comes but once a year.

It seems that Thomas Tusser and Omar Khayyam shared a similar temperament. Both men loved poetry, the heavens, and the earth, and they both took delight in the simple pleasures of life. Tusser loved the four seasons just as much as Khayyam loved the stars. Tusser loved planting the soil and taking care of animals, while Khayyam clearly loved playing number games.

Take a closer look at another one of Tusser's poems. Notice that he wrote it in quatrains, or poems of four lines, just like Omar Khayyam. The rhyming pattern is slightly different, however. It follows an *AABB* pattern in which the first two lines rhyme with each other and the last two lines rhyme with each other. Mark the ends of the lines of this poem accordingly as you read through it.

The stone that is rolling, can gather no moss,	A
Who often removeth is surer of loss;	A
The rich it compelleth to pay for his pride,	B
The poor it undoeth, on every side.	B

▶ Think about what this poem means. You may have heard the proverb "The rolling stone gathers no moss." What does Tusser mean by quoting this proverb in his poem? Can moss grow on a stone that is always moving?

Tell It Back—**Narration**

Narrate the biography of the poet that you chose to study. Begin with the first line of the biography. Choose a few choice words that the description used and include them in your own narration.

Talk About It—

1. Do you remember what figurative language is? Whenever you describe something by comparing it with something else, you are using figurative language. Khayyam uses the wilderness figuratively by suggesting that life can be like a wilderness when it is difficult or bleak. How does Tusser use the image of a stone figuratively? Just as the wilderness means something different than a thorny desert, the stone means something different than a rock.

2. How do the lives of Thomas Tusser and Omar Khayyam provide a good example of enjoying simple pleasure and honest work?

3. What is useful about Khayyam's saying: "Wilderness is paradise enough"? What is useful about Tusser's saying: "The stone that is rolling, can gather no moss"?

4. Can you think of any individual in history or in a story who wasted his life by fooling around too much? (This is the contrast portion of the chreia.)

5. Can you think of an individual you know who works hard and enjoys the simple pleasures of life? (This is the comparison portion of the chreia.)

Go Deeper—

Mark the rhyming patterns in the poems that follow. Give a different letter to each rhyme sound, but note that some rhymes are not exact, such as "temperate" and "date."

A. Little Boy Blue, come blow your horn.

The sheep's in the meadow, the cow's in the corn.

Where is the boy that looks after the sheep?

"He's under the haycock, fast asleep."

Will you wake him? "No, not I;

For if I do, he'll be sure to cry."

B. To market, to market, to buy a fat pig,

Home again, home again, dancing a jig;

To market, to market, to buy a fat hog;

Home again, home again, jiggety-jog;

To market, to market, to buy a plum bun,

Home again, home again, market is done.

C. There was a young lady from Niger

Who smiled as she rode on a tiger;

They returned from the ride

With the lady inside,

And the smile on the face of the tiger.

D. I think that I shall never see

A poem lovely as a tree.

A tree whose hungry mouth is prest

Against the earth's sweet flowing breast;

A tree that looks at God all day,

And lifts her leafy arms to pray;

A tree that may in summer wear

A nest of robins in her hair;

Upon whose bosom snow has lain;

Who intimately lives with rain.

Poems are made by fools like me,

But only God can make a tree.

E.   'Twas the night before Christmas, when all through the house

Not a creature was stirring, not even a mouse;

The stockings were hung by the chimney with care,

In hopes that St. Nicholas soon would be there;

The children were nestled all snug in their beds;

While visions of sugar-plums danced in their heads;

And mamma in her 'kerchief, and I in my cap,

Had just settled our brains for a long winter's nap,

When out on the lawn there arose such a clatter,

I sprang from my bed to see what was the matter.

F.   Little Miss Muffet

Sat on a tuffet,

Eating her curds and whey;

Along came a spider,

Who sat down beside her,

And frightened Miss Muffet away.

Writing Time—

1. **DICTATION**—Your teacher will read a quote from a poem by Thomas Tusser. Please listen carefully! After your teacher reads once, she will read slowly again and include the punctuation marks and line breaks. Your task will be to write down the lines as your teacher reads them one by one.

_____

_____

_____

_____

2. **SENTENCE PLAY**—Here's a chance for you to play the poet like Tusser or Khayyam. Rhyme with the first lines provided by using one of the rhyming words in parentheses to write a second line.

Example: There was a Young Lady whose chin, _____. (pin/thin)
There was a Young Lady whose chin,
Resembled the point of a pin.

a. There was an Old Man in a boat,

_____. (goat/float)

b. There was an Old Man on a hill,

_____. (still/ill)

c. There was a Young Person of Crete,

_____. (feet/treat)

d. There once were some very large rats

_____. (hats/cats)

e. There was a Young Lady whose eyes

_____. (size/pies)

3. **COPIOUSNESS**—

A. Subjects and predicates (the action part of a sentence) can be made more poetic with descriptive words such as adjectives and adverbs. Using the following subjects and predicates, build sentences that include at least one adjective and one adverb. Sentences may be as long or as short as you like. Examples:

SUBJECT: poet   PREDICATE: wrote

The lazy poet wrote busily.

The lazy poet wrote busily after his morning coffee.

SUBJECT: poet   PREDICATE: planted

The gardening poet planted joyfully.

The gardening poet planted joyfully in the good earth of his farm.

i. SUBJECT: farmer   PREDICATE: milked

_____

ii. SUBJECT: moon   PREDICATE: rises

_____

iii. SUBJECT: clowns   PREDICATE: fell

_____

iv. SUBJECT: climbers   PREDICATE: will go

_____

v. SUBJECT: monsters   PREDICATE: lurk

_____

B. Use the following adverbs to create sentences. Make sure your subjects are specific and your verbs are active. There is a suggested topic in parentheses if you need one to get started. If you have your own topic, that's fine too. Remember that adverbs describe how, where, when, and how often something happens.

Examples: Adverb: moodily

The willow trees swayed moodily in the stormy breeze.

Adverb: bright

The moon burned bright in the night.

i. quickly (Khayyam solving math problems)

_____

_____

ii. slowly (Tusser tilling the soil)

_____

_____

iii. accidentally (a diver slipping)

_____

_____

iv. usually (belching)

_____

_____

v. happily (a dog running)

_____

_____

C. Add a prepositional phrase to the beginning or end of the following sentences using the preposition in the parentheses. Remember that prepositions are often short words that show a time or space connection between words. A prepositional phrase begins with a preposition; for example, "against all odds" or "down by the bank."

Example: Tusser pulled the crops _____. (from)
Change to: Tusser pulled the crops from the field.

i. _____

_____, the pirate was forced to walk the plank. (at)

ii. What is the name _____

_____? (of)

iii. _____

_____, many galaxies are waiting to be discovered. (beyond)

iv. The basketball player ran _____

_____. (around)

4. **CHREIA**—Write your own chreia about Omar Khayyam or Thomas Tusser by following the steps listed.

Paragraph 1—Praise Omar Khayyam or Thomas Tusser. Show how the poet lived his life according to the principles in his poems.

_____

_____

_____

_____

_____

_____

_____

_____

_____

_____

_____

Paragraph 2—Give a new version of one of the author's poems. Use your own words to rephrase the poem to show that you understand it. (No rhyming is necessary.)

_____

_____

_____

_____

_____

_____

_____

_____

Paragraph 3—Why is this poem's saying useful? Give details to support your answer.

_____

_____

_____

_____

_____

_____

_____

_____

Paragraph 4—Introduce a contrast. Think of an example of someone in history or in a story who did not enjoy life or who fooled around too much. Give your example in the form of a very short narrative or story.

_____

_____

_____

_____

_____

_____

_____

_____

Paragraph 5—Introduce a comparison. Now think of an example of someone you know personally who works hard and enjoys the simple pleasures of life. Give your example in the form of a very short narrative or story.

_____

_____

_____

_____

_____

_____

_____

_____

_____

_____

Paragraph 6—Conclude with a brief epilogue. Remember, an epilogue is nothing more than a tidy ending for your essay. It is like the ribbon on a present that wraps up everything neatly. You can use your own life as an example or conclude with any other relevant thoughts.

_____

_____

_____

_____

_____

_____

_____

_____

_____

5. **IMITATION**—

   a. Try writing a poem to fit the rhyming pattern of one of the poems from the *Rubaiyat*: *AABA*.

      Example: Ah, my Beloved, fill the Cup that clears   A

      To-day of past Regrets and future Fears—   A

      To-morrow?—Why, To-morrow I may be   B

      Myself with Yesterday's Sev'n Thousand Years.   A

_____

_____

_____

_____

   b. Create a last line for the following Robert Frost quatrain, which has a rhyming pattern of *AABA*. Some suggested rhyming words are included in parentheses.

      My little horse must think it queer

      To stop without a farmhouse near

      Between the woods and frozen lake

      _____

      (year, tear, sneer, fear, dear, steer, deer, spear)

   c. Try writing a poem that imitates the rhyming pattern (*AABB*) of this Thomas Tusser quatrain:

      North winds send hail, South winds bring rain,

      East winds we bewail, West winds blow amain;

      North-east is too cold, south-east not too warm,

      North-west is too bold, south-west doth no harm.

Thomas Tusser wrote in a form of English that was perfect for the sixteenth century, but we rarely use words like "doth" and "amain" nowadays. Use modern words to write your own poem. You could write again about winds and create your own rhyme, such as "North winds bring snow, South winds bring fog," or you could write about trees, such as "Pear trees bear fruit, Maple trees give sap." Or, write about something else you know well—pets, animals, sports, and so on.

_____

_____

_____

_____

Speak It—

Before this lesson, you had probably never heard of the poets Tusser or Khayyam. Most Americans are first introduced to poetry through nursery rhymes. When we hear them as adults we feel glad because they return us to the early pleasure of hearing the rhythms and rhymes of poetry.

Whatever Americans know about the Middle Ages often comes from nursery rhymes as well. Many of these little poems come to us from very old songs, riddles, and proverbs that were eventually compiled in the eighteenth century. The following rhymes are adapted from *Mother Goose's Melody* by John Newbery. Although Mother Goose is the imaginary author, her character is probably based on the many medieval women who made up the rhymes for their children.

Work with your classmates to learn the following rhymes and perform them for an audience.

Lesson 8: Fifth Chreia—Two Medieval Poets: Omar Khayyam and Thomas Tusser

About mills

There was an old woman
Lived under a hill,
She put a mouse in a bag,
And sent it to mill.
The miller did swear,
By the point of his knife,
He never took toll
Of a mouse in his life.

There was an old woman,
And she sold puddings and pies:
She went to the mill,
And the dust flew in her eyes:
Hot pies and cold pies to sell!
Wherever she goes,—
You may follow her by the smell.

About the importance of cats

Ding Dong Bell,
The cat is in the well.
Who put her in?
Little Johnny Green.
What a naughty boy was that,
To drown a poor Pussy cat,
Who never did any harm
And kill'd the mice in his father's barn.

Pussy cat, pussy cat, where have you been?
I've been down to London to visit the Queen.
Pussy cat, pussy cat, what did you there?
I frightened a little mouse, under her chair.

About market day

Ride a cock-horse

To Banbury Cross,

To see what Tommy can buy;

A penny white loaf,

A penny white cake,

And a two-penny apple-pie.

This little pig went to market

This little pig stayed at home;

This little pig had roast meat,

That little pig had none.

This pig went to the barn-door,

And cry'd week, week, for more.

Bah, Bah a black Sheep,

Have you any Wool?

Yes marry have I,

Three Bags full;

One for my master,

One for my Dame,

But none for the little Boy

Who cries in the lane.

To market, to market, to buy a fat pig,

Home again, home again, jiggety-jig.

To market, to market, to buy a fat hog,

Home again, home again, jiggety-jog.

To market, to market, to buy a plum bun,

Home again, home again, market is done.

Lesson 9 · · · · · · · · · ·

Sixth Chreia— Francis of Assisi

Saint Francis, or Francis of Assisi, was born to a wealthy family and spent his youth feasting and drinking with the other young men of Assisi, Italy. It was only after Francis joined a military expedition against a neighboring Italian state that he learned about suffering and death. After a year of captivity, he returned home a changed man. He pledged his life to helping the poor and the needy and established a new order of begging friars, the Little Brothers. According to biographer Paul Sabatier, "He went . . . to the sick, the forgotten, the disdained. He dispensed the treasures of his heart according to the need and reserved the best of himself for the poorest and the most lost, for lepers and thieves." Take a look at some of the stories of Francis's kindness in the following narrative.

Francis of Assisi, 1181–1226

adapted from *Fifty Famous People* by James Baldwin and *Life of St. Francis of Assisi* by Paul Sabatier

Not to hurt our humble brethren is our first duty to them. —Francis of Assisi

Francis was riding on horseback one day, his mind more than ever filled with the desire to lead a life of absolute devotion to God, when at a turn of the road he found himself face to face with a **leper**. The frightful disease of **leprosy** had always inspired in him an invincible revulsion. He could not control a movement of horror, and he quickly turned his horse and rode off in another direction.

If the shock of seeing the leper had been severe, he felt far worse running away from him. He blamed himself bitterly. Here he wanted to do such wonderful, noble things, and yet, when put to the test, he showed himself so cowardly! He retraced his steps and, springing from his horse, he gave to the astounded leper all the money that he had. Then he kissed the leper's hand as he would have done to a priest.

Another time a poor man approached one of the Little Brothers, asking for **alms**. The Brother said to him, "How can I be sure that you are truly in need? Perhaps you are a rich man pretending to be poor. Why should I believe you?" When Francis, who was often called "the father of the poor," heard this, he was deeply saddened. He reprimanded the Brother and told him to strip off his habit before the poor man and beg for forgiveness and also to ask the poor man to pray for him.

Very kind and loving was Saint Francis. He was kind and loving not only to men but to all living things. He spoke of the birds as his little sisters of the air, and he could never bear to see them harmed. At Christmastime he scattered crumbs of bread under the trees so that the tiny creatures could feast and be happy.

Many stories are told of Francis's great love and pity for the timid creatures that lived in the fields and woods. Once Saint Francis encountered a boy who was on his way to market to sell a pair of doves he had snared. Francis said to the boy, "These are innocent birds, which are compared in scripture to chaste and faithful souls. I beg you earnestly not to put them into the hands of persons who would kill them, but to **confide** them to me."

Lesson 9: Sixth Chreia—Francis of Assisi

The boy not only gave Saint Francis the doves, but he also joined the Franciscan friars in their work for the poor. Meanwhile, Francis made a nest for the doves, and the mother bird laid her eggs in it. By and by, the eggs hatched, and a nestful of young doves grew up. They were so tame that they sat on the shoulders of Saint Francis and ate from his hand.

On another day, as he was walking among the trees, the birds saw him and flew down to greet him. They sang their sweetest songs to show how much they loved him. Then, when they saw that he was about to speak, they nestled softly in the grass and listened.

"O little birds," he said, "I love you, for you are my brothers and sisters of the air. Let me tell you something, my little brothers, my little sisters: You ought always to love God and praise Him.

"For think what He has given you. He has given you wings with which to fly through the air. He has given you clothing both warm and beautiful. He has given you the air in which to move and have homes.

"And think of this, O little brothers: You sow not, neither do you reap, for God feeds you. He gives you the rivers and the brooks from which to drink. He gives you the mountains and the valleys where you may rest. He gives you the trees in which to build your nests.

"You toil not, neither do you spin, yet God takes care of you and your little ones. It must be, then, that He loves you. So, do not be ungrateful, but sing His praises and thank Him for his goodness toward you."

Then the saint stopped speaking and looked around him. All the birds sprang up joyfully. They spread their wings and opened their mouths to show that they understood his words. And when he had blessed them, they all began to sing, and the whole forest was filled with sweetness and joy because of their wonderful melodies.

Saint Francis will always be remembered for his kindness to animals and to poor people as well. He was always eager to preach good news to the suffering and bind up the brokenhearted. He was quick to remind rich and powerful people that "not to hurt our humble brethren is our first duty to them."

Tell It Back—Narration

Without looking at the text, tell the story of Saint Francis as best you remember it using your own words and keeping the details in order. Try to sprinkle your telling with a few of the author's words, such as "leprosy," "revulsion," and "alms." Here is the first sentence to get you started: "Francis was riding on horseback one day, his mind more than ever filled with the desire to lead a life of absolute devotion to God, when at a turn of the road he found himself face to face with a leper."

Talk About It—

1. What are some words you could use to describe Saint Francis? Why?

2. What is the meaning of Saint Francis's saying: "Not to hurt our humble brethren is our first duty to them"? How is this saying useful to us today?

3. Can you think of anybody in history or in a story who is known for his cruelty to people or animals? (This is the contrast portion of the chreia.)

4. Can you think of anybody in history or in a story or someone from your life who is known for his kindness to people or animals? (This is the comparison portion of the chreia.)

Go Deeper—

For each question, circle or supply the correct answer(s).

1. Our word "animal" comes from the Latin word *animal*. It is related to the Latin word *anima*, which means "wind," "air," "breath," "life," and even "soul" or "spirit." Animals have the "breath of life" in them. From *anima* we get our word "animate," which means "to give life to" or "to make alive" and as an adjective means "possessing life" or "lively." From *anima* we also get the word "inanimate," which means "lifeless," "sluggish," or "dull." Which of the

following phrases best describe something that is literally or figuratively animated? (See lesson 2 for definitions of "literal" and "figurative.")

a. a movie with cartoons that move

b. a rambunctious puppy

c. a pumpkin pie

d. a lifelike stone sculpture

2. The word "saint" comes from the Latin word *sanctus*, which means "holy." A holy person is sometimes called a saint. A holy place can be called a sanctuary. Can you name some other famous saints?

_____

_____

_____

_____

3. A leper is a person with a fearsome skin and nerve disease. What do you suppose a *leper colony* is?

a. a group of insects

b. government buildings built for sick people

c. a group of people with leprosy who are living away from other people

d. a weak nation ruled by a stronger nation

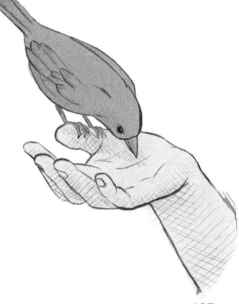

4. What type of story is the story of Saint Francis? (Circle all that apply.)

   a. myth

   b. saint story

   c. legend

   d. fable

   e. history

Writing Time—

1. **DICTATION**—Your teacher will read a quote from the narrative about Saint Francis. Please listen carefully! After your teacher reads once, she will read slowly again and include the punctuation marks. Your task will be to write down the sentences as your teacher reads them one by one.

   _____

   _____

   _____

2. **SENTENCE PLAY**—<u>One time a poor man approached one of the Little Brothers, asking for alms.</u> Notice how the second part of the sentence, with a verb ending in *-ing*, fits with the first part of the sentence. The phrase in the second part of the sentence adds to the information in the beginning of the sentence; it explains for what reason the poor man approached the brother. The poor man asked for alms, which is money given to help the poor.

   How would the second part of the sentence change if a rich man approached the Little Brother instead? Perhaps it would read like this: "One time a rich man approached one of the Little Brothers, showering him with money."

   Look at another example, this time with two verbs: "One time a sick child approached one of the Little Brothers, coughing like crazy and sneezing up a storm." In this case, the phrase that makes up the second part of the sentence describes what the sick child is doing.

In the following exercise, complete the second part of each sentence (beginning with an -ing word) based on who approaches one of the Little Brothers.

a. One time a strong man approached one of the Little Brothers, carrying

_____.

b. One time a crying child approached one of the Little Brothers, saying,

"_____."

c. One time a police officer approached one of the Little Brothers, _____

_____.

d. One time a lion approached one of the Little Brothers, _____

_____.

Now try using two verbs with -ing endings.

Example: One time a robber approached one of the Little Brothers, pointing a sword and saying, "Give me all your candy, if you please."

e. One time a farmer approached one of the Little Brothers, _____

_____.

f. One time a grandmother approached one of the Little Brothers, _____

_____.

Now choose who will approach the Little Brother in addition to supplying the -ing phrase.

g. One day a _____ approached one

of the Little Brothers, _____.

3. **COPIOUSNESS**—Remember that there are many ways to say the same thing. That's what copiousness is all about. Your writing will be more interesting if you know how to express yourself in a variety of ways.

A. Label the one noun and three verbs in the following sentence:

The birds saw him and flew down to greet him.

i. Change this sentence by adding a prepositional phrase to the beginning of it. Prepositional phrases begin with words such as "in," "to," "up," "for," "after," "from," "under," and "before." For example, "in the barn," "over the moon," or "around the city."

_____,

the birds saw him and flew down to greet him.

ii. Use synonyms to change the three verbs of this sentence. (You may replace the adverb "down" with a different adverb if necessary.)

_____

_____

iii. Use two adjectives to describe the birds and also make the noun ("birds") a more specific word. (A specific bird, for instance, would be a robin.)

_____

_____

iv. Move the adverbial phrase "down to greet him" to the beginning of the sentence and rewrite the sentence to both make sense and to keep nearly the same meaning.

_____

_____

v. Change the active voice ("the birds saw") in the first half of the sentence to passive voice, in which the subject is acted upon by the birds.

_____

_____

         N   V

B. The <u>boy</u> not only <u>gave</u> Saint Francis the

     N   V

<u>birds</u>, but he also <u>joined</u> the

                   N   N

Franciscan friars in their <u>work</u> for the <u>poor</u>.

i. Replace all underlined verbs and common nouns in this sentence with synonyms.

_____

_____

ii. Change all verbs in active voice to passive voice, starting with "The doves . . ."

_____

_____

iii. Move the prepositional phrases "in their work for the poor" to the beginning of the sentence and rewrite the sentence to keep the same meaning.

In their work for the poor, _____

_____.

4. **CHREIA**—Write your own chreia about Saint Francis by following the steps listed.

Paragraph 1—Praise Saint Francis. Show how he lived his life according to the principles in his saying.

_____

_____

_____

_____

_____

_____

_____

_____

_____

Paragraph 2—Give a new version of the saying "Not to hurt our humble brethren is our first duty to them." Use your own words to rephrase the saying to show that you understand it.

_____

_____

_____

_____

Lesson 9: Sixth Chreia—Francis of Assisi

Paragraph 3—Why is this saying useful? Give details to support your answer.

_____

_____

_____

_____

_____

_____

_____

_____

_____

Paragraph 4—Introduce a contrast. Think of an example of someone in history or in a story who was cruel to people or to animals. Give your example in the form of a very short narrative or story.

_____

_____

_____

_____

_____

_____

_____

_____

Paragraph 5—Introduce a comparison. Now think of an example of someone in history or in a story who was kind to people or to animals. Give your example in the form of a very short narrative or story.

_____

_____

_____

_____

_____

_____

_____

_____

_____

_____

Paragraph 6—Conclude with a brief epilogue. Remember, an epilogue is nothing more than a tidy ending for your essay. It is like the ribbon on a present that wraps up everything neatly. You can use your own life as an example or conclude with any other relevant thoughts.

_____

_____

_____

_____

_____

Lesson 9: Sixth Chreia—Francis of Assisi

_____

_____

_____

_____

5. **IMITATION OF A MONOLOGUE**—Here is what Saint Francis said to the birds:

"O little birds, I love you, for you are my brothers and sisters of the air. Let me tell you something, my little brothers, my little sisters: You ought always to love God and praise Him.

"For think what He has given you. He has given you wings with which to fly through the air. He has given you clothing both warm and beautiful. He has given you the air in which to move and have homes.

"And think of this, O little brothers: You sow not, neither do you reap, for God feeds you. He gives you the rivers and the brooks from which to drink. He gives you the mountains and the valleys where you may rest. He gives you the trees in which to build your nests.

"You toil not, neither do you spin, yet God takes care of you and your little ones. It must be, then, that He loves you. So, do not be ungrateful, but sing His praises and thank Him for his goodness toward you."

Using a similar style, write a gentle and loving speech to cats, to dogs, or to goldfish as if they could understand what you are saying. Consider speaking it earnestly. Remember that even in our own culture we have horse and dog "whisperers" who are good at working with animals and seem to be able to understand and communicate (at some level) with them.

_____

_____

_____

_____

_____

_____

_____

_____

_____

_____

_____

Speak It—

Deliver your speech to cats, dogs, or goldfish to your classmates, or record yourself on a recording device. Or, memorize and recite to your class the following famous poem attributed to Saint Francis:

The Prayer of Saint Francis

Lord, make me an instrument of Your peace;

Where there is hatred, let me sow love;

Where there is injury, pardon;

Where there is error, truth;

Where there is doubt, faith;

Where there is despair, hope;

Where there is darkness, light;

And where there is sadness, joy.

O Divine Master, Grant that I may not so much seek

To be consoled as to console;

To be understood as to understand;

To be loved as to love;

For it is in giving that we receive;

It is in pardoning that we are pardoned;

And it is in dying that we are born to eternal life.

Lesson 10

Seventh Chreia— Queen Elizabeth I

Queen Elizabeth I came to power in 1558, a difficult time in the history of England. Her island kingdom lay near several enemy states, each determined to see her off the throne. Even worse for Elizabeth, the citizens of her own country were divided against each other: Protestant against Catholic, Catholic against Protestant. They were on the brink of a civil war.

The unity of Christianity, which had lasted for many centuries, had come to an end with the Reformation, one of the most turbulent periods of church history. Protestants, protesting certain Catholic beliefs and practices, broke away from the Roman Catholic Church and formed new churches. One of these new Protestant churches was the Church of England, which came under the leadership of the king or queen of England.

It was indeed a challenging time to assume leadership of a country. The most frightening episode during that time was an invasion from Catholic Spain by a huge fleet of ships known as the Spanish Armada. What follows is the story of that armada.

Queen Elizabeth I, 1533–1603

—adapted from *In the Days of Queen Elizabeth* by Eva March Tappan

Cowards falter, but danger is often overcome by those who nobly dare.
—Queen Elizabeth I

An Englishman living in Lisbon, Portugal, hastened home to England and demanded an audience with the queen. "Your Majesty," he said, "King Philip II of Spain is making great preparations for some warlike enterprise. In the Lisbon harbor are twenty **galleons** and forty other vessels. Soldiers from Italy and Germany are coming in by hundreds. What can this mean but an attack upon England?"

Two months later came a message to the queen from her spies in Spain: "Soldiers are coming every day, and vast quantities of wine, grain, biscuit, bacon, oil, vinegar, barley meal, and salted meats are being laid in besides powder and cannon."

A ship that had recently sailed from Lisbon was captured by the English, and both captain and men were tortured on the rack so that more might be learned of the doings of Philip. All told the same story, that Philip was planning an invasion of England.

Philip II of Spain was indeed determined to attack England. Queen Mary was dead, and he claimed the crown by virtue of his connection with the royal house of Lancaster and by the will of the queen of Scotland.

There was another side to his plan as well. Elizabeth had helped to tear her country from its allegiance to the pope. If Philip conquered England, the country would be brought back to the Roman Catholic Church, and so would Holland. A Spanish cardinal wrote, "Spain does not war against Englishmen, but against Elizabeth. It is not England but her wretched queen who has overthrown the Holy Church and persecuted the pious Catholics. Let the English people rise and welcome their deliverer." This letter was circulated throughout England, but it produced no effect except to increase the loyalty of English Catholics to their queen.

The wildest stories spread across the country of what the Spaniards would do once they were in control of the kingdom. It was said that they had already lists of the stately castles of the realm and the homes of rich London merchants, marked with the names of the Spanish nobles to whom they were to be given. Most of the English were to be hanged, so the rumor went, but all children under seven years of age were to be branded on the face and kept as slaves. These stories were not true, but they stirred the English people up against Spain.

While the shipbuilders of Spain were working night and day, and while men and provisions and powder and cannon were being brought together, England too was preparing for the encounter. There was no ally on the continent of Europe to lend aid. The fortifications of the kingdom were weak. At Portsmouth the guns had not been able to be fired when the queen was crowned because the tower was so old and ready to crumble, and for thirty years little had been done to put it in order.

However, this very weakness of the resources of the government became England's strength, for every Englishman saw that if his country was to be saved from becoming a province of Spain, he and every other man must do his best to defend it.

The queen's advisors sent a message to London: "What number of ships and men is it your wish to contribute to the defense of the land?"

"How many may properly be required of us?" asked the Londoners.

"Fifteen ships and five thousand men," was the answer.

Now in all London there were hardly more than seventeen thousand men, but the city straightway wrote to the council: "Ten thousand men and thirty ships we will gladly provide, and the ships shall be amply furnished."

So it was throughout the kingdom. Every town sent a generous number of men and generous gifts of money. Every little village on the coast hastened to refit its fishing vessels and offer boats and sailors to the government.

Philip had not expected to conquer England with only the aid of the soldiers whom he was to carry with him. He had a large band of allies on English soil, so he thought, waiting for his coming and ready to welcome him. These were the Catholics of England. The Pope had, after all, **excommunicated** Elizabeth.

"These are not common days," said one of Elizabeth's advisers, "and in such times there must often be resort to means that would be most cruel and unjust in other years."

"What do you mean?" demanded the queen.

"Your Majesty has, of course, not failed to consider the support that the Spanish king may find if he succeeds in landing upon our shores."

"Who will support him, you or I?"

"It would be but natural for those of his own church to welcome him."

"They'll welcome him with powder and cannon. What would you have me do, cut off the heads of my faithful subjects? I rule men and women, not their thoughts, and if a man obeys me, his head stays on his shoulders, mark that. I'll tell you one thing more: The lord high-admiral of my fleet is to be Howard of Effingham. What think you of that, my man?"

"But, your Majesty, he is a strong supporter of the Catholic faith."

"So will he be of the queen," replied Elizabeth calmly.

The queen appointed Howard admiral and Sir Francis Drake, the great explorer, vice-admiral.

The English vessels came together. There were all sorts of craft, ranging from a ship not much smaller than the galleons of the Spaniards to small craft hardly more than fishing boats. They were miserably supplied with food and powder.

When the Invincible Armada had left Spain, Admiral Howard wrote, "If the wind holds out for six days, Spain will be knocking at our doors."

Sure enough, the Spanish ships slowly made their way into the English Channel. They were so large and so high at stem and stern that they looked like great floating castles. And yet, they were so clumsy and difficult to manage that the nimble little English boats had a great advantage. The Spanish fleet formed in a wide crescent, the two points seven miles apart, and the English boats went out to meet them.

The galleons were high and the English vessels so low that it was difficult to train the Spanish guns upon them. Moreover, the Spaniards were not good marksmen. They would have had a better chance if the English had only been willing to stand still and be fired at, but the Spanish were much surprised and disgusted when the saucy little English craft slipped up under their very bows, fired a shot or two, and were away firing at the next ship before the Spanish guns could be trained upon them. Some of the little boats sailed the whole length of the crescent, firing at every vessel and coming off without a scar.

This kind of encounter was kept up for more than a week, for the English hesitated to attempt a regular engagement. The Spanish suffered severely. Masts were shattered, the rigging was cut up, great, ragged holes were torn in the hulls, and large numbers of sailors were slain, but even worse was to follow when they retreated from England.

Following their retreat, the Spaniards were anchored off the French port of Calais. At two o'clock one morning a strange, shapeless object was seen floating toward them. Then came another and another until there were eight. Fire blazed up from the floating monsters. There were explosions and suffocating gases. The flames rose higher; wind and waves were bringing these malignant creatures that seemed half alive into the midst of the Spanish fleet.

This attack by fire-boats was a new way of fighting. The Spaniards were perplexed and horrified. Their only thought was to escape anywhere, no matter where, if only they could get free from these terrors. In their haste, anchor chains fouled, some ships collided, and others burned or ran aground.

The English land forces were encamped at Tilbury. "I am commander in chief of my troops," declared Elizabeth, "and I shall go to pay them a visit."

"Is it safe to commit yourself to armed multitudes? Among so many there may well be treachery," suggested her councilors.

"Let tyrants fear," returned Elizabeth. "I am true to my people, and they are my faithful and loving subjects. I should rather die than live in fear and distrust of them. I shall go to visit my loyal soldiers."

It must have been a brilliant sight, the long lines of soldiers in battle array and the queen riding in front of the lines on her great charger. Before her went the Earl of Leicester and another noble bearing the sword of state. Behind her followed a page carrying her helmet with its white plumes. She was magnificently dressed, but over her dress was a **corslet** of polished steel. Back and forth before the lines she rode, while the soldiers shouted, "Queen Elizabeth! Queen Elizabeth! God save the queen! The Lord keep her!" She raised her hand, and there was silence to hear her words.

"I have the body of a woman," she said, "but I have the heart of a king, of a king of England, and I think it foul scorn that any prince of Europe should dare to invade the borders of my realm. Rather than that any dishonor should come by me, I will take up arms. I will be your general myself, and the rewarder of every deed of bravery. You deserve already rewards and crowns, and they shall be paid. It will not be long before we have a famous victory over these enemies of my kingdom and of my people."

In the end, England won a great victory. The Spanish ships ran aground on the unknown coasts. They were shattered by storms, the sailors were stricken by disease, and they were driven ashore only to be thrust back into the waves. Of the great fleet that left Spain, so strong that it had ventured to call itself invincible, more than half the ships were left on the rocks or at the bottom of the sea.

Queen Elizabeth had been put to the test, and she had proved herself to be courageous. Today historians regard her as one of the greatest monarchs of all time. Her words still ripple across the waters of time: "Cowards falter, but danger is often overcome by those who nobly dare."

Tell It Back—Narration

This is a long narrative—the longest you have encountered in the Writing & Rhetoric series yet! Together with your class, see if you can outline the major events in the story. Be sure that someone is writing them down to keep track.

Talk About It—

1. What did Queen Elizabeth mean by "Cowards falter, but danger is often overcome by those who nobly dare"?

2. In what ways did Elizabeth show herself to be daring and courageous in this story from her life?

3. Can you think of anybody in history or in a story who showed cowardice in the face of danger? (This is the contrast portion of the chreia.)

4. Can you think of anybody in history or in a story who overcame his fears and showed great courage in the face of danger? (This is the comparison portion of the chreia.)

Go Deeper—

For each question, circle or supply the correct answer(s).

1. The English word "cowardice" comes from the Latin word *cauda*, which means "tail." A frightened dog will drop its tail, tuck it between its legs, and "cower" away. Someone who flees from danger or confrontation can be called a coward, and that kind of behavior can be called cowardice. Have you seen any other examples of cowardice in your life?

   _____

   _____

   _____

   _____

   _____

   _____

2. Which of the following are examples of cowardice or cowardly behavior?
   a. running away from a fire and not telling anyone
   b. eating dinner very slowly
   c. laughing about a serious matter
   d. not standing up for a friend who is being unfairly criticized
   e. a soldier who runs away during a battle

3. Which of the following words describe the opposite of cowardice or cowardly behavior? You may look up words you do not know in the dictionary.
   a. courage
   b. bravery
   c. kindness
   d. fearlessness
   e. humility
   f. valor
   g. daring

4. Our English word "majestic" comes from the Latin word *maiestas*, which means "greatness," "dignity," and "majesty." Kings and queens were called "Your Majesty" because of the greatness of their positions, even if they were not very good kings or queens. What kind of things do you call majestic?

_____

_____

_____

Writing Time—

1. **DICTATION**—Your teacher will read a quote from the narrative about Queen Elizabeth. Please listen carefully! After your teacher reads once, she will read slowly again and include the punctuation marks and line breaks. Your task will be to write down the sentence as your teacher reads it.

_____

_____

_____

_____

2. **SENTENCE PLAY**—

   A. <u>Soldiers are coming every day, and vast quantities of wine, grain, biscuit, bacon, oil, vinegar, barley meal, and salted meats are being laid in.</u> Using this sentence as a model, write new sentences in the same style. Note that this sentence contains two statements joined by the word "and." A list of items forms the subject of the second statement.

   Example: Camping takes lots of planning, and tents, sleeping bags, ground pads, matches, firewood, bug spray, sunblock, and food are all important to pack.

Lesson 10: *Seventh Chreia—Queen Elizabeth I*

The following are some ideas for topics:

- things Queen Elizabeth packed to take on her journey to the soldiers
- things to take to the beach
- things to get out of storage for a holiday
- items to use during a blackout

i. _____

_____

_____

ii. _____

_____

_____

iii. _____

_____

_____

B. <u>Masts were shattered, the rigging was cut up, great, ragged holes were torn in the hulls, and large numbers of sailors were slain.</u> Using this sentence as a model, write new sentences in the same style. Note that this sentence is really a list of related events and that each part is separated by commas.

Example: Potatoes were mashed, the turkey was carved, cold, sweet cranberry sauce was spooned up, and everyone sat down to eat.

The following are some ideas for topics:

- Queen Elizabeth's decision to go to the front and meet her soldiers
- how a food dish or dessert is made
- how a football, hockey, lacrosse, or other game is played
- the order of events in a book or movie

i. _____

_____

_____

ii. _____

_____

_____

iii. _____

.

_____

3. **COPIOUSNESS**—Here is another opportunity for you to put Erasmus's advice—"Write, write, and again write"—into practice. Rarely settle for the first draft of anything. Always push yourself to use more specific words.

◀ *Armada Portrait* of Queen Elizabeth I by George Gower

A. Examine the Armada portrait of Queen Elizabeth I by the painter George Gower. This painting celebrates the English victory over Spain and shows off the power and wealth of England. The following descriptions of this painting are weak. Using the prompts provided, write a more interesting version of each sentence.

Elizabeth's dress is very fancy.

Think of comparisons that would give a better picture of the dress. These comparisons, using "like" or "as," are known as similes.

Examples: Elizabeth's dress is like a puff pastry decorated with frosting.
Elizabeth's dress is as fancy as a peacock's feathers.

i. Elizabeth's dress is like _____

_____.

ii. Elizabeth's dress is as fancy as _____

_____.

B. The following description tells almost nothing about the lace that you see in the painting. Is the lace stiff, straight, limp, or wrinkled? Is it white, pink, or sepia-toned? Does it surround the queen's neck or hang down in front like a cravat or tie? Give a detailed description of the lace using color, texture, and other observations. Then complete the similes.

There is lace around the queen's neck.

i. Description: _____

_____

_____

ii. Elizabeth's lace surrounds her neck like _____

_____

_____.

iii. Elizabeth's lace is as white as _____

_____

_____.

4. **CHREIA**—Write your own chreia about Queen Elizabeth by following the steps listed.

Paragraph 1—Praise Queen Elizabeth. Show how she lived her life according to the principles in her saying: "Cowards falter, but danger is often overcome by those who nobly dare."

_____

_____

_____

_____

_____

_____

_____

Paragraph 2—Give a new version of the saying "Cowards falter, but danger is often overcome by those who nobly dare." Use your own words to rephrase the saying to show that you understand it.

_____

_____

_____

Lesson 10: *Seventh Chreia—Queen Elizabeth I*

Paragraph 3—Why is this saying useful? Give details to support your answer.

_____

_____

_____

_____

_____

_____

_____

Paragraph 4—Introduce a contrast. Think of an example of someone in history or in a story who was cowardly in the face of danger. Give your example in the form of a very short narrative or story.

_____

_____

_____

_____

_____

_____

_____

Paragraph 5—Introduce a comparison. Now think of an example of someone who showed courage in the face of danger. It could be someone you know. Give your example in the form of a very short narrative or story.

_____

_____

_____

_____

_____

_____

_____

Paragraph 6—Conclude with a brief epilogue. Remember, an epilogue is nothing more than a tidy ending for your essay. It is like the ribbon on a present that wraps up everything neatly. You can use your own life as an example or conclude with any other relevant thoughts.

_____

_____

_____

_____

_____

_____

_____

Speak It—

No speaker worth her salt would give a speech without taking her audience into account. Would you word your speech the same for a classroom of kindergarteners as for seniors in high school? Would you give the same delivery to an audience of clowns as you would to an audience of pirates? Would you give a speech about never looking sad at a funeral? The answers are obvious. Speakers must tailor their speeches to the needs of their audiences. When Queen Elizabeth spoke to the audience of soldiers, she tailored her speech to their situation. If Elizabeth had given the same speech to a group of loyal subjects back at home, it would have been inappropriate and very clear that she did not know to whom she was speaking.

Do you know the story of the Pied Piper? The Piper came to the village of Hamelin to help the townsfolk clear out an infestation of rats. He played his pipe, and all the rats followed him into a river. Modify the following short speech by the Pied Piper to make it suitable for the different audiences listed. In the original speech, the Piper is speaking to the mayor of the town and his council, the richest townsfolk.

"Please, your honors, I'm able, by means of a secret charm, to draw all creatures by playing my pipe. Chiefly I use my music to carry away creatures that do people harm: moles and toads, newts and vipers. In Tartary, I freed the people from a swarm of gnats. In Asia, I swept away a huge cloud of vampire bats. Will you give me a thousand gold coins if I pipe away your rats?"

Pick two of the following possible audiences and rewrite the Pied Piper's speech two different ways so that it makes sense for those particular audiences. Feel free to change the wording, including the species of animals listed, as long as the general meaning is kept intact. Then share your new speeches aloud with your classmates.

- an audience of toddlers
- an audience of cowboys
- an audience of ballerinas
- an audience of farmers
- an audience of musicians
- an audience of exterminators (people who are already in the job of killing animal pests)
- an audience of animal lovers

1. _____

_____

_____

_____

_____

_____

_____

_____

_____

2. _____

_____

_____

_____

_____

_____

_____

_____

_____

Lesson 11

Eighth Chreia—
Lady Godiva

Chreias are not only written about useful sayings. They can also be written about useful actions. When someone has done something particularly brilliant or memorable, writers may want to praise the doer and examine the action so that future generations can learn from it.

When you write a chreia about a useful action, you follow the same steps as a chreia about a saying: Praise the doer. Examine why the deed was useful. Introduce a contrast and a comparison. Write an epilogue. (You don't need to rewrite actions as you did the sayings, so that part of the essay will be missing.)

In the following section, take a look at a story about one person whose action was worthy of praise.

Lady Godiva, c. 1040–1070

Lady Godiva was a real person whose name and property can be found listed in the *Domesday Book* of 1086, which was a survey that listed all English landholders of the period. Her famous action is only a legend, however, and while it proved useful in her situation, I don't recommend that you try it in your hometown!

Godiva's husband was the Earl of Mercia, a powerful lord in the Danish nobility who had conquered England. According to the legend, Earl Leofric was ruthlessly taxing his Saxon subjects. Godiva, a Saxon herself, pleaded with her husband to take less money, but he scorned her concern. He told her that he'd tax the people less only if she had the courage to ride through the streets of Coventry naked.

During the time of William the Conqueror, men were sent all over England to make a record of the property of landholders. William used the record book to discover who was important and rich in his newly conquered kingdom. He gave away many parcels of land to the Norman warriors who battled with him against the Saxons. The cheated Saxon landholders (or thanes) were deeply resentful, and the *Domesday Book* only cemented their second-class status.

Godiva took him up on his challenge. She assured him that the Saxon people were honorable and would shutter their windows rather than gawk at her. What follows is the story as told in the poem *Godiva* by Alfred, Lord Tennyson. In the end, there was one man who peeped at Lady Godiva and lost his eyesight; he became known as Peeping Tom.

The woman of a thousand summers back,
Godiva, wife to that grim Earl, who ruled
In Coventry: for when he laid a tax
Upon his town, and all the mothers brought
Their children, clamoring, "If we pay, we starve!"
She sought her lord, and found him, where he strode
About the hall, among his dogs, alone,
His beard a foot before him and his hair
A yard behind. She told him of their tears,
And pray'd him, "If they pay this tax, they starve."
Whereat he stared, replying, half-amazed,
"You would not let your little finger ache

For such as these?"—"But I would die," said she.

He laugh'd, and swore by Peter and by Paul;

Then **fillip'd** at the diamond in her ear;   flicked

"Oh ay, ay, ay, you talk!"—"Alas!" she said,

"But prove me what I would not do."

And from a heart as rough as Esau's hand,

He answer'd, "Ride you naked thro' the town,

And I repeal it;" and nodding, as in scorn,

He parted, with great strides among his dogs.

So left alone, the passions of her mind,

As winds from all the compass shift and blow,

Made war upon each other for an hour,

Till pity won. She sent a herald forth,

And bade him cry, with sound of trumpet, all

The hard condition; but that she would loose

The people: therefore, as they loved her well,

From then till noon no foot should pace the street,

No eye look down, she passing; but that all

Should keep within, door shut, and window barr'd.

Then fled she to her inmost **bower**, and there   an enclosed place

Unclasp'd the wedded eagles of her belt,

The grim Earl's gift; but ever at a breath

She linger'd, looking like a summer moon

Half-dipt in cloud: anon she shook her head,

And shower'd the rippled ringlets to her knee;

Unclad herself in haste; adown the stair

Stole on; and, like a creeping sunbeam, slid

From pillar unto pillar, until she reach'd

The Gateway, there she found her **palfrey trapt**   light saddle horse; dressed

In purple **blazon'd** with armorial gold.   adorned

Then she rode forth, clothed on with **chastity**:   purity

The deep air listen'd round her as she rode,

And all the low wind hardly breathed for fear.

The little wide-mouth'd heads upon the spout

Had cunning eyes to see: the barking **cur**   aggressive dog

Made her cheek flame; her palfrey's foot-fall shot

Light horrors thro' her pulses; the blind walls

Were full of chinks and holes; and overhead

Fantastic **gables**, crowding, stared: but she   triangular roofs

Not less thro' all bore up, till, last, she saw

The white-flower'd elder-thicket from the field,

Gleam thro' the Gothic archway in the wall.

Then she rode back, clothed on with chastity;

And one low **churl**, compact of thankless earth,   rude, lowly person

The fatal **byword** of all years to come,   common phrase

Boring a little **auger**-hole in fear,   drilling tool

Peep'd—but his eyes, before they had their will,

Were shrivel'd into darkness in his head,

And dropt before him. So the Powers, who wait

On noble deeds, cancell'd a sense misused;

And she, that knew not, pass'd: and all at once,

With twelve great shocks of sound, the shameless noon

Was clash'd and hammer'd from a hundred towers,

One after one: but even then she gain'd

Her bower; whence reissuing, robed and crown'd,

To meet her lord, she took the tax away

And built herself an everlasting name.

Tell It Back—Narration

- Without looking at the text, tell the story of Lady Godiva's ride through town
as best you remember it using your own words and keeping the details in order.
Try to sprinkle your telling with a few of the carefully chosen words of the poet's
that are your favorites, words such as "ringlets," "palfrey," and "peeped."

Talk About It—

1. What was useful about Lady Godiva's action? Who are the shameful people in this story?

2. Would people find Godiva's action shocking today? Would people today be honorable enough to shutter their windows?

3. Can you think of anybody in history or in a story who was greedy or who taxed people too much? (This is the contrast portion of the chreia.)

4. Can you think of anybody in history or in a story who tried to help the poor or who resisted tyranny such as excessive taxation? (This is the comparison portion of the chreia.)

Go Deeper—

For each question, circle or supply the correct answer(s).

1. Compare the story of Lady Godiva to the one in the previous chapter about the courage of Queen Elizabeth. Did Lady Godiva act in ways similar to Queen Elizabeth? In what ways were Lady Godiva's actions different from those of Queen Elizabeth?

_____

_____

_____

_____

_____

2. What do you think about the character of the earl, who suggested that his wife ride naked through the town?

_____

_____

_____

_____

3. What else might you guess is true of the earl given what you know about him from his actions and the description of him in the poem? Circle all that apply.

   a. He was greedy.

   b. He cared about power.

   c. He cared about his wife.

   d. He loved his people.

   e. He was self-sacrificing.

   f. He was willing to listen to his people.

4. Write an alternative title that you think would be appropriate for this story.

   _____

   _____

5. Lady Godiva believed that the townspeople would shutter their windows rather than *gawk* at her. The word "gawk" probably means which of the following? Circle all the words that apply.

   a. peer

   b. talk

   c. gaze

   d. stare

   e. discuss

Lesson 11: Eighth Chreia—Lady Godiva

Writing Time—

1. **DICTATION**—Your teacher will read a quote from the poem about Lady Godiva. Please listen carefully! After your teacher reads once, she will read slowly again and include the punctuation marks and line breaks. Your task will be to write down the sentences as your teacher reads them one by one.

_____

_____

_____

2. **SENTENCE PLAY**—<u>Like a creeping sunbeam, she slid from pillar unto pillar.</u> This sentence contains the lovely simile "like a creeping sunbeam." Remember that a simile is a comparison using "like" or "as." This simile describes the secretive way that Lady Godiva sneaked downstairs to get outside unseen.

What else can you think of that slides or glides, flits or tiptoes? In the following exercise, use other comparisons to show how Lady Godiva slid from object to object.

Example: Like raindrops on glass, she slid from pillar unto pillar.

a. _____

b. _____

c. _____

3. **COPIOUSNESS**—

A. <u>If we pay, we starve.</u> This is what the mothers of Coventry said to the Earl of Mercia. Think of three different ways to express the same concern. Use synonyms, or expand the sentence by adding nouns, adjectives, adverbs, and prepositional phrases, rearrange the clauses, use passive voice, and so on. Use a thesaurus only if you get stuck.

Examples:

Using synonyms: If we give money, we go hungry.

Rearranging **clauses**: We starve if we pay.

Adding adverbs: If we pay everything, we will starve quickly.

Adding nouns and adjectives: If you take our silver coins, we die of horrid starvation and thirst.

i. _____

ii. _____

iii. _____

B. <u>The barking of a dog made her cheek flame.</u> Think of three different ways to express the same sentence. Use synonyms, expand the sentence by adding nouns, adjectives, adverbs, and prepositional phrases, rearrange the clauses, use passive voice, and so on.

Keep in mind that a flaming cheek is figurative language that suggests embarrassment. Lady Godiva was embarrassed when the dog barked because it reminded her that someone might be seeing her as she rode through the streets without clothes. You may make this part of the sentence literal or use your own figurative language.

Example: The woofing dog caused her cheeks to burn hot.

i. _____

ii. _____

iii. _____

4. **CHREIA**—Write your own chreia about Lady Godiva by following the steps listed.

Paragraph 1—Praise Lady Godiva for her concern for the poor and her willingness to take action.

_____

_____

_____

_____

_____

_____

Paragraph 2—Why was Lady Godiva's action useful? Give details to support your answer.

_____

_____

_____

_____

_____

_____

Paragraph 3—Introduce a contrast. Think of an example of someone in history or in a story who used his power to be greedy. Give your example in the form of a very short narrative or story.

_____

_____

_____

_____

_____

_____

_____

_____

Paragraph 4—Introduce a comparison. Now think of an example of someone who fought against tyranny, oppression, or corruption. Give your example in the form of a very short narrative or story.

_____

_____

_____

_____

_____

_____

Lesson 11: Eighth Chreia—Lady Godiva

Paragraph 5—Conclude with a brief epilogue. Remember, an epilogue is nothing more than a tidy ending for your essay. It is like the ribbon on a present that wraps up everything neatly. You can use your own life as an example or conclude with any other relevant thoughts.

_____

_____

_____

_____

_____

_____

_____

_____

_____

Speak It—

Divide Tennyson's *Godiva* into parts and use it to create a dramatic reading, recitation, or pageant for parents or other students.

> The woman of a thousand summers back,
>
> Godiva, wife to that grim Earl, who ruled
>
> In Coventry: for when he laid a tax
>
> Upon his town, and all the mothers brought
>
> Their children, clamoring, "If we pay, we starve!"
>
> She sought her lord, and found him, where he strode
>
> About the hall, among his dogs, alone,
>
> His beard a foot before him and his hair
>
> A yard behind. She told him of their tears,
>
> And pray'd him, "If they pay this tax, they starve."

Whereat he stared, replying, half-amazed,

"You would not let your little finger ache

For such as these?"—"But I would die," said she.

He laugh'd, and swore by Peter and by Paul;

Then fillip'd at the diamond in her ear;

"Oh ay, ay, ay, you talk!"—"Alas!" she said,

"But prove me what I would not do."

And from a heart as rough as Esau's hand,

He answer'd, "Ride you naked thro' the town,

And I repeal it;" and nodding, as in scorn,

He parted, with great strides among his dogs.

So left alone, the passions of her mind,

As winds from all the compass shift and blow,

Made war upon each other for an hour,

Till pity won. She sent a herald forth,

And bade him cry, with sound of trumpet, all

The hard condition; but that she would loose

The people: therefore, as they loved her well,

From then till noon no foot should pace the street,

No eye look down, she passing; but that all

Should keep within, door shut, and window barr'd.

Then fled she to her inmost bower, and there

Unclasp'd the wedded eagles of her belt,

The grim Earl's gift; but ever at a breath

She linger'd, looking like a summer moon

Half-dipt in cloud: anon she shook her head,

And shower'd the rippled ringlets to her knee;

Unclad herself in haste; adown the stair

Stole on; and, like a creeping sunbeam, slid

From pillar unto pillar, until she reach'd

Lesson 11: Eighth Chreia—Lady Godiva

The Gateway, there she found her palfrey trapt

In purple blazon'd with armorial gold.

Then she rode forth, clothed on with chastity:

The deep air listen'd round her as she rode,

And all the low wind hardly breathed for fear.

The little wide-mouth'd heads upon the spout

Had cunning eyes to see: the barking cur

Made her cheek flame; her palfrey's foot-fall shot

Light horrors thro' her pulses; the blind walls

Were full of chinks and holes; and overhead

Fantastic gables, crowding, stared: but she

Not less thro' all bore up, till, last, she saw

The white-flower'd elder-thicket from the field,

Gleam thro' the Gothic archway in the wall.

Then she rode back, clothed on with chastity;

And one low churl, compact of thankless earth,

The fatal byword of all years to come,

Boring a little auger-hole in fear,

Peep'd—but his eyes, before they had their will,

Were shrivel'd into darkness in his head,

And dropt before him. So the Powers, who wait

On noble deeds, cancell'd a sense misused;

And she, that knew not, pass'd: and all at once,

With twelve great shocks of sound, the shameless noon

Was clash'd and hammer'd from a hundred towers,

One after one: but even then she gain'd

Her bower; whence reissuing, robed and crown'd,

To meet her lord, she took the tax away

And built herself an everlasting name.

Keys for an effective dramatic reading or recitation:

1. Thoroughly review the poem so that every actor understands it.

2. Each speaking character should develop a unique voice for the dialogue sections and use that voice consistently. The narrator, while sounding more **NEUTRAL**, should still use emotional inflection, varying volume, and speed.

3. Use hand gestures, but don't overdo it. Too much action on stage can distract from the words.

4. Find the emotional climax—the high point—of the poem and make sure the volume is punched up there.

5. Costumes or props and a nice backdrop will add interest to the recitation.

Lesson 12

Ninth Chreia— King Richard III

Unlike Alfred the Great and Queen Elizabeth I, King Richard III is not thought of highly by many people in Great Britain. Some historians claim that he murdered his brother's two young sons in order to steal the throne from them. He was supposed to be their protector, but instead he locked them away in the Tower of London, where they disappeared from history. Richard III's short reign of two years was blemished by revolts and the executions of traitors. Later, Shakespeare would make him a bloodthirsty and deformed villain in his play *Richard III*.

After you read the following narrative about Richard III and the Battle of Bosworth Field, you will examine an anonymous proverb based on that story. (The proverb is printed at the beginning of the narrative.) An anonymous proverb has no author that can be identified. No one will ever know who first came up with the saying.

King Richard III, 1452–1485

For want of a nail the shoe was lost;

For want of a shoe the horse was lost;

For want of a horse the battle was lost;

For the failure of battle the kingdom was lost—

All for the want of a horse-shoe nail.

In England, in 1485, a blacksmith was shoeing an illustrious horse.

"Shoe him quickly, for the king wishes to ride him to battle," said the groom who had brought the horse.

"Do you think there will be a battle?" asked the blacksmith.

"Most certainly, and very soon, too," answered the man. "The king's enemies are even now advancing, and all are ready for the fight. Today will decide whether Richard or Henry shall be king of England."

The smith went on with his work. From a bar of iron he made four horseshoes. These he hammered and shaped and fitted to the horse's feet. Then he began to nail them on. But after he had nailed on two shoes, he found that he had not nails enough for the other two.

"I have only six nails," he said, "and it will take a little time to hammer out ten more."

"Oh, well," said the groom, "won't six nails do? Put three in each shoe. I hear the trumpets now. King Richard will be impatient."

"Three nails in each shoe will hold them on," said the smith. "Yes, I think we may risk it."

So he quickly finished the shoeing, and the groom hurried to lead the horse to the king.

The battle had been raging for some time. King Richard rode hither and thither, cheering his men and fighting his foes. His enemy, Henry, who wished to be king, was pressing his army hard.

Far away, at the other side of the field, King Richard saw his men falling back. Without his help they would soon be beaten, so he spurred his horse to ride to their aid.

He was hardly halfway across the stony field when one of his horse's shoes flew off. The horse was lamed on a rock. Then another shoe came off. The horse stumbled, and his rider was thrown heavily to the ground.

Before the king could rise, his frightened horse, although lame, had galloped away. The king looked and saw that his soldiers were beaten and that the battle was everywhere going against him.

He waved his sword in the air and shouted, "A horse! A horse! My kingdom for a horse!"

But there was no horse for him. His soldiers were intent on saving themselves. They could not give him any help.

Eventually the battle was lost. King Richard was lost, and Henry, the Duke of Richmond, became king of England.

Tell It Back—Narration

Without looking at the text, tell the story of King Richard losing his kingdom, starting with the shoeing of his horse. Include some details about his character that come from the short historical introduction. Tell the story as best you remember it using your own words and keeping the details in order.

Talk About It—

1. What do you think is the moral of this story? In other words, what does the figurative language of the proverb mean?

2. How would you describe Richard III from his portrait? Use specific words to describe him.

3. Thomas More described Richard III this way: "Richard, the third son, was . . . little of stature, ill-featured of limbs, crooked-backed, his left shoulder much higher than his right, hard-favored in appearance, and such as is in the

▲ Late sixteenth-century portrait of Richard III

case of lords called warlike, in other men called otherwise. He was malicious, wrathful, envious, and from before his birth, ever perverse." The author seems to be making a connection between Richard III's physical appearance and his behavior. Is this fair?

4. Can you think of any incident in history or in a story when good preparation saved the day? (This is the contrast portion of the chreia.)

5. Can you think of any incident in history or in a story when carelessness caused a disaster? (This is the comparison portion of the chreia.)

Go Deeper—

For each question, circle or supply the correct answer(s).

1. The Latin word *paro* means "to get ready" or "to set." The Latin word *praeparo* means "to get ready beforehand," or ahead of time. It is from *praeparo* that we get our word "prepare." The Boy Scouts have as their motto "Always prepared." Which of the following words come close to the meaning of "prepared"?
   a. ready
   b. interested
   c. rehearsed
   d. able
   e. groomed

2. Which of the following words or phrases come close to meaning the opposite of being prepared? You may use a dictionary for the words you do not know.
   a. hard-working
   b. unready
   c. unable
   d. tired
   e. delighted
   f. unprepared

3. The story behind the anonymous saying in this lesson is historical, and yet it has an antagonist and conflict like almost all narratives do. Who is the antagonist, and what is the conflict in this story?

_____

_____

_____

_____

_____

4. The story in this lesson illustrates the importance of focusing on details and the ruin that comes from ignoring them. But what would happen if the king got stuck thinking only of the picky little details? What are some of the bigger ideas and matters that are important if a king wants to defend his kingdom and win a battle?

_____

_____

_____

_____

_____

_____

Writing Time—

1. **DICTATION**—Your teacher will read a quote from the narrative about Richard III. Please listen carefully! After your teacher reads once, she will read slowly again and include the punctuation marks. Your task will be to write down the sentences as your teacher reads them one by one.

_____

_____

_____

_____

2. **SENTENCE PLAY**—

   A. He shouted, "A horse! A horse! My kingdom for a horse!" How would this plea for help change in a different circumstance? If a girl were terribly thirsty, for example, her shout may go something like this: "Some water! Some water! My smartphone for some water!"

   With the underlined sentence serving as a model, create similar sentences using the topics listed.

   i. A snowman wants a hat.

   _____

   _____

   ii. A cowgirl wants some baked beans.

   _____

   _____

   iii. A spider wants a fly.

   _____

   _____

iv. Now create a sentence using your own topic.

_____

_____

B. <u>"Shoe him quickly, for the king wishes to ride him to battle," said the groom who had brought the horse.</u> How would this command change in a different circumstance? If a servant brought a bowl of cherries to a baker, the sentence might read like this: "Crush these quickly, for the king wishes to eat a cherry pie," said the servant who had brought a bowl of cherries.

With the underlined sentence serving as a model, create similar sentences using the topics listed.

i. A hunter brings a venison steak to the cook.

_____

_____

ii. A fairy godmother brings glass slippers to Cinderella.

_____

_____

iii. A gardener brings flowers to the maid.

_____

_____

3. **COPIOUSNESS**—

A. <u>The king wishes to ride the horse to battle.</u> Think of three different ways to express the same statement. Use synonyms, expand the sentence by adding nouns, adjectives, adverbs, and prepositional phrases, rearrange the clauses, use passive voice, and so on. Use a thesaurus only if you get stuck.

Example: His Majesty wants to gallop upon the horse into war.

i. _____

_____

ii. _____

_____

iii. _____

_____

B. <u>"Do you think there will be a battle?" asked the blacksmith.</u> The blacksmith could have asked this question a number of different ways. For example, he could have said, "Do you suppose there will be warfare?" Think of three different ways to express the same question. Use synonyms, expand the sentence by adding nouns, adjectives, adverbs, and prepositional phrases, rearrange the clauses, and so on. Use a thesaurus only if you get stuck.

_____

_____

_____

_____

_____

_____

4. **CHREIA**—Write your own chreia about the anonymous proverb by following the steps listed.

Paragraph 1—Praise the anonymous saying itself.

For want of a nail the shoe was lost;

For want of a shoe the horse was lost;

For want of a horse the battle was lost;

For the failure of battle the kingdom was lost—

And all for the want of a horse-shoe nail.

_____

_____

_____

_____

_____

_____

_____

_____

_____

_____

_____

Paragraph 2—Give a new version of the proverb. Use your own words to rephrase the saying to show that you understand it.

_____

_____

_____

_____

_____

Paragraph 3—Why is this proverb useful? Give details to support your answer.

_____

_____

_____

_____

_____

_____

_____

_____

_____

Paragraph 4—Introduce a contrast. Think of an example of an incident in history or in a story when careful preparation prevented disaster. Give your example in the form of a very short narrative or story.

_____

_____

_____

_____

_____

_____

_____

Lesson 12: *Ninth Chreia—King Richard III*

Paragraph 5—Introduce a comparison. Now think of an example of an incident in history or in a story when carelessness caused a disaster. Give your example in the form of a very short narrative or story.

_____

_____

_____

_____

_____

_____

_____

Paragraph 6—Conclude with a brief epilogue. Remember, an epilogue is nothing more than a tidy ending for your essay. It is like the ribbon on a present that wraps up everything neatly. You can use your own life as an example or conclude with any other relevant thoughts.

_____

_____

_____

_____

_____

_____

_____

5. **IMITATION**—Use the proverb "For want of a nail" as a model and write a new proverb showing a chain of events in four stages.

For example: For want of a bolt the chain was lost,

For want of the chain the tire was lost,

For want of the tire the bike was lost,

For want of the bike the biker was lost,

And all for want of a paltry bolt.

_____

_____

_____

_____

_____

Speak It—

Research one of the well-known types of horses used during the Middle Ages in the following list. These horses were identified by the jobs they performed. Then use index cards to write and deliver an informational speech to your class. Draw a picture of the horse for use as a visual aid during your talk.

- Draft horse—the largest horse, used to pull siege weapons
- Destrier or great horse—large horse used to carry knights in heavy armor and used in battle or tournaments
- Courser (charger)—a war horse, not as heavy as the destrier, but faster; had good endurance and was also prized as a hunting horse
- Rouncey—a lighter horse used by squires or knights' assistants, also useful in pursuing game
- Palfrey—a riding and hunting horse favored by women
- Hobby or jennet—a light horse used for scouting, spying, and lightly armored cavalry

Elocution Instructions

Whether you are reciting a poem or delivering a speech, you want to speak in such a way that the audience can hear you "loud and clear." The art of speaking skillfully is known as elocution. So, what goes into proper elocution?

First of all, you should make sure you are pronouncing all of your words clearly. This means you are making each word sharp and crisp instead of blending them together and mumbling.

Second, good posture is very important for speaking loudly enough. You can't breathe very well if you are slouched over. Stand up straight and tall, square your shoulders, and look at your audience. Look directly into their eyes. This will help your listeners know that you are a confident speaker. They will enjoy your recitation more when they see how confident you are.

Finally, don't speak too quickly. It's hard to understand a recitation that blasts off like a rocket ship. You will want to speak at a good pace and pause every now and then to let your words sink in.

In addition, practice speaking with:

- volume. Everyone in the room should be able to hear you.
- drama. You should sound sad when the words call for sorrow, angry when the words call for anger. Any emotion in the text should find its way into your voice.
- gestures. Gestures accentuate the emotions in your voice and make the reading even more dramatic.
- pauses and proper speed. Never read quickly without taking a breath. Pauses help to emphasize your emotions just as gestures also help to emphasize emotions.

You will delight your listeners if you can stand up straight, look into their eyes, and speak loudly and clearly at just the right pace. As you practice speaking skillfully, your writing will improve. And as your writing improves, your speaking will also improve—they work together.

Logos and Lexis

Ancient educators taught us nearly everything we know about rhetoric, the practice of persuasive speaking. Aristotle noted two important parts of rhetoric: *logos* and *lexis*. *Logos* is Greek for "word" and also for "logical reasoning." So *logos* is the content, the substance of a speech. It's what you put down on paper and the words that are spoken. *Lexis* is the delivery of the words, how the speech comes across to the audience.

Both *logos* and *lexis* are important for effective public speaking. We might call them substance and style today. The content of a speech can mean the difference between sharing excellent ideas or spouting stuff and nonsense. The way you use your voice in speaking can mean the difference between catching the interest of your audience or putting them to sleep.

What are some ways to make the delivery, or *lexis*, of a speech more interesting? You already know that proper volume—loudness and softness—is vital to *lexis*. Speed—not speaking too fast or too slowly—is also key. In addition to proper volume and speed, there is also inflection. What is inflection?

Think about the different ways you could say the words, "I'd like to have you for dinner." If you say this sentence in a nice, casual voice, it sounds as if you are inviting someone to your house for a meal. If you say it sarcastically, it sounds like you really don't want her to come over for dinner. If you say it in a raspy, wolfish voice, it sounds as if you want to eat someone up. The change in the pitch or tone of your voice is called inflection.

In order to hold your audience's attention, you are going to need to use the highs and lows of your voice. Inflection tells the audience when they need to be excited or when they should laugh or get serious. It is the emotion added to your voice. It gives your words meaning. We know that when a person asks us a question, his voice will get a little higher at the end of his sentence. We know when we're about to hear bad news because a person's voice goes lower. A good speaker will know how to use inflection to make his speech more powerful and more meaningful.

Proper elocution is an important aspect of *lexis*. You may write the most incredible speech, but without good speaking skills—without good *lexis*—your speech will not make a strong impact on your audience. So practice your elocution, practice your *lexis*, until you have them down!

Glossary

Literary and Rhetorical Concepts

Active voice—the subject does the action of the action verb (e.g., The spider ate the fly.)

Adjective—describes a noun and helps us to "see" it more clearly: e.g., happy, silly, strange

Adverb—usually describes a verb and answers the questions "how?", "when?", and "where?"; can also describe adjectives or other adverbs

Biography—a description of someone's life

Character—a person who has a role to play in a story

Chreia—a short essay or remembrance that praises the author of a saying or the doer of an action and shows why the saying or action is useful

Clause—a group of words within a sentence containing a subject and a verb

Copiousness—stretching exercises for students of rhetoric whereby students reach for new words to express variations of the same idea*

Dialogue—a conversation between two or more people

Elocution—the art of public speaking

Epilogue—a tidy ending to a written work

Fable—a short story that teaches a simple moral lesson, usually with talking animals

Figurative language—wording that suggests an imaginative meaning that goes beyond what the actual words say

Full rhyme—rhymes that share many of the same letters or have exactly the same sounds

Inflection—the change in pitch or tone of the voice that is used to make spoken words more meaningful

*A broad definition of copiousness is any large quantity or number. Food, birds, or bubbles can be copious. In rhetoric, copiousness is aimed at developing a richness and flexibility of language so that many words and many ways of phrasing those words are available to the writer and speaker.

Legend—a story that begins with a real person or event that, as it is handed down by storytellers, often gets exaggerated along the way; a person who is so remarkable that he becomes extremely famous

Lexis—the manner of delivery of a speech

Literal—the ordinary or factual meaning of a word or saying

Logos—the content of a speech

Memorize—to learn something by heart

Monologue—a long speech by one person or character

Moral—the short lesson that explains the meaning of a fable

Narrative—all forms of story, from fairy tale, to history, to myths, to parables, to fables

Noun—a person, place, thing, or idea: e.g., astronaut, island, sled, love

Outline—the skeleton of a story that tells what comes in the beginning, the middle, and the end

Parable—a short story that teaches a moral lesson, always true to life

Paragraph—a group of sentences that form an idea together

Passive voice—the subject is acted upon by the action verb (e.g., The fly was eaten by the spider.)

Point of view—a way of seeing things

Predicate—the part of speech that tells what the subject of a sentence does

Preposition—a word that connects a noun or a pronoun to the sentence and shows location (position), direction, or time: e.g., over, under, to, from, inside, and outside

Prepositional phrase—a phrase that begins with a preposition: e.g., over the moon, toward the castle, after midnight

Proverb—a wise saying or a short, clever insight into human behavior

Rhetoric—the art and practice of persuasive writing and speaking

Rhyme—similar sounds repeated close to each other in poetry

Simile—a comparison using the words "like" or "as"

Slant rhyme—rhymes that are more distant, without the exact letters or sounds repeated, but still have a similarity between them

Subject—what the sentence is about

Synonym—a word that has nearly the same meaning as another word

Topic sentence—the sentence that tells what the paragraph is about

Verb—the action word of a sentence

Vocabulary Builder

Alms—gifts of food or money to the poor

Amain—at full speed

Auger—drilling tool

Avalanche—a huge slide of rocks or snow falling down a mountain

Blazon'd—adorned

Bough—a branch of a tree

Bower—a shady or enclosed place in a garden or wood

Byword—an often-used phrase, e.g., Peeping Tom

Chastity—purity

Chivalry—a code of behavior for knights

Chreiodes—useful

Churl—rude, lowly person

Clave—stuck closely to (past tense of "cleave")

Confide—to entrust, or to tell a secret to someone

Corslet—a piece of armor covering the trunk of the body

Cur—a dog that is aggressive or in poor condition

Enow—enough

Excommunicated—the state of being removed from the fellowship of a church and unable to receive Holy Communion

Fillip'd—flicked

Gable—triangular roof

Galleon—heavy sailing ship with three masts and multiple levels

Hospitality—kindness to guests

Husbandry—an old-fashioned way to say "taking care of a farm"

Ignorance—a lack of knowledge and education

Leper—someone who is afflicted with leprosy

Leprosy—a disease that attacks a person's nerves and skin and leaves him disfigured; curable today, but was terrifying to people for thousands of years

Neutral—objective or unbiased

Overthrow—to bring down or to conquer

Palfrey—a light saddle horse

Persona non grata—an unwelcome person

Prowess—great skill

Redressing—setting right

Respe—raspberries

Scullions—lowly kitchen servants

Silk—a smooth and shiny fiber used to make comfortable clothes

Trapt—dressed

So Long, Farewell, Adiós, Good-bye

You've worked hard at your chreias, I presume, and if so you've certainly earned a breather. Breathe in deeply. Now let the air out slowly. Nice job.

But, wait! Before you go, take a moment to reflect on what you've learned these past few weeks. It's never advisable to plunge blindly through your education without taking time to see how far you've come. That would be like climbing a mountain and taking no time to admire the view from the top.

Probably the most important skill you learned is how to create paragraphs. A paragraph is a group of sentences that form an idea together. When we communicate, we organize our thoughts so that we can do it clearly, and paragraphs are one of the ways we organize our thoughts on paper. You also learned that the most important sentence in each paragraph is called the topic sentence. This is the sentence that tells us what the paragraph is about. Everything you ever write will use paragraphs. Narrative paragraphs don't need topic sentences, but you will need topic sentences when you write essays.

"More!" you say. "Surely I learned more than that!" But of course you did! You learned to write a specific type of six-paragraph essay called a chreia, which is a short remembrance of something useful someone said or did.

▶ Can you remember what was included in each paragraph of the chreia?

You also learned that a proverb is a wise saying or a short, clever insight into human behavior. Many proverbs use both literal and figurative language. With literal language, what you see is what you get—the words mean exactly what they say. When somebody says, "I just got hit by a ball," that somebody means, "I just got hit by a ball." Figurative language uses words to express another meaning. "An idea just hit me" means that an idea just entered a person's brain. The word "hit" is used figuratively because it doesn't really mean a slap or a punch.

In addition, you reviewed the concepts of *logos* and *lexis*, which are important for effective public speaking. *Logos* is Greek for "word," and also for "logical reasoning." So *logos* is the content, the substance of a speech. It's what you put down on paper and the words that are spoken. *Lexis* is your style, the kind of words you use and how your speech comes across to the audience.

I would venture to guess that you also learned a lot about some pretty interesting human beings, yes? I hope so. History is full of stories and interesting people we can learn from, and I hope this book has whet your appetite for more adventures in writing. Perhaps we will meet again in the next book in this series, *Writing & Rhetoric, Book 5: Refutation & Confirmation*. In this new book, you will learn to have an argument without fussing, yelling, or screaming, and that is something well worth learning, don't you think?

And now, on that note, I must really take my leave with one last proverb: "Every good-bye brings the next hello a little closer." So until we meet again, *adieu*.

So Long, Farewell, *Adiós*, Good-bye

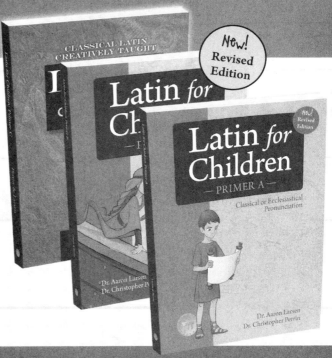

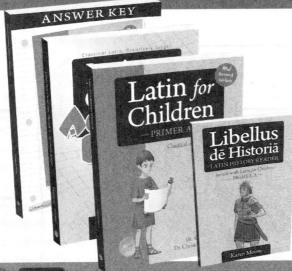